Philadelphia Phillies 2020

A Baseball Companion

Edited by R.J. Anderson, Craig Goldstein and Bret Sayre

Baseball Prospectus

Craig Brown, Steven Goldman and David Pease, Consultant Editors
Robert Au, Harry Pavlidis and Amy Pircher, Statistics Editors

Copyright © 2020 by DIY Baseball, LLC.
All rights reserved

This book or any part thereof may not be reproduced or transmitted in any form or by any means, electronic or mechanical, including photocopying, recording, or by any information storage and retrieval system, without permission in writing from the publisher.

Limit of Liability/Disclaimer of Warranty: While the publisher and the author have used their best efforts in preparing this book, they make no representations or warranties with respect to the accuracy or completeness of the contents of this book and specifically disclaim any implied warranties of merchantability or fitness for a particular purpose. No warranty may be created or extended by sales representatives or written sales materials. The advice and strategies contained herein may not be suitable for your situation. You should consult with a professional where appropriate. Neither the publisher nor the author shall be liable for any loss of profit or any other commercial damages, including but not limited to special, incidental, consequential, or other damages.

Library of Congress Cataloging-in-Publication Data:
paperback
ISBN-13: 978-1-950716-12-8

Project Credits
Cover Design: Michael Byzewski at Aesthetic Apparatus
Interior Design and Production: Jeff Pease, Dave Pease
Layout: Jeff Pease, Dave Pease

Baseball icon courtesy of Uberux, from https://www.shareicon.net/author/uberux

Ballpark diagram courtesy of Lou Spirito/THIRTY81 Project, https://thirty81project.com/

Manufactured in the United States of America
10 9 8 7 6 5 4 3 2 1

Table of Contents

Statistical Introduction v

Part 1: Team Analysis

Philadelphia Phillies: Where Are You Going, Where Have You Been? . . . 3
  Justin Klugh, Jarrett Seidler and Matthew Trueblood
Performance Graphs 11
2019 Team Performance 12
2020 Team Projections 13
Team Personnel 14
Citizens Bank Park Stats 15
Phillies Team Analysis 17

Part 2: Player Analysis

Phillies Player Analysis 24
Phillies Prospects 105

Part 3: Featured Articles

The Baseball Is Juiced (Again) 123
  Robert Arthur
The Moral Hazard of Playing It Safe 127
  Craig Goldstein

Index of Names 133

Statistical Introduction

Sports are, fundamentally, a blend of athletic endeavor and storytelling. Baseball, like any other sport, tells its stories in so many ways: in the arc of a game from the stands or a season from the box scores, in photos, or even in numbers. At Baseball Prospectus, we understand that statistics don't replace observation or any of baseball's stories, but complement everything else that makes the game so much fun.

What stats help us with is with patterns and precision, variance and value. This book can help you learn things you may not see from watching a game or hundred, whether it's the path of a career over time or the breadth of the entire MLB. We'd also never ask you to choose between our numbers and the experience of viewing a game from the cheap seats or the comfort of your home; our publication combines running the numbers with observations and wisdom from some of the brightest minds we can find. But if you *do* want to learn more about the numbers beyond what's on the backs of player jerseys, let us help explain.

Offense

We've revised our methodology for determining batting value. Long-time readers of the book will notice that we've retired True Average in favor of a new metric: Deserved Runs Created Plus (DRC+). Developed by Jonathan Judge and our stats team, this statistic measures everything a player does at the plate–reaching base, hitting for power, making outs, and moving runners over–and puts it on a scale where 100 equals league-average performance. A DRC+ of 150 is terrific, a DRC+ of 100 is average and a DRC+ of 75 means you better be an excellent defender.

DRC+ also does a better job than any of our previous metrics in taking contextual factors into account. The model adjusts for how the park affects performance, but also for things like the talent of the opposing pitcher, value of different types of batted-ball events, league, temperature and other factors. It's able to describe a player's expected offensive contribution than any other statistic we've found over the years, and also does a better job of predicting future performance as well.

There's a lot more to DRC+'s story, and you can read all about it in greater depth near the end of this book.

The other aspect of run-scoring is baserunning, which we quantify using Baserunning Runs. BRR not only records the value of stolen bases (or getting caught in the act), but also accounts for all the stuff that doesn't show up on the back of a baseball card: a runner's ability to go first to third on a single, or advance on a fly ball.

Defense

Where offensive value is *relatively* easy to identify and understand, defensive value is…not. Over the past dozen years, the sabermetric community has focused mostly on stats based on zone data: a real-live human person records the type of batted ball and estimated landing location, and models are created that give expected outs. From there, you can compare fielders' actual outs to those expected ones. Simple, right?

Unfortunately, zone data has two major issues. First, zone data is recorded by commercial data providers who keep the raw data private unless you pay for it. (All the statistics we build in this book and on our website use public data as inputs.) That hurts our ability to test assumptions or duplicate results. Second, over the years it has become apparent that there's quite a bit of "noise" in zone-based fielding analysis. Sometimes the conclusions drawn from zone data don't hold up to scrutiny, and sometimes the different data provided by different providers don't look anything alike, giving wildly different results. Sometimes the hard-working professional stringers or scorers might unknowingly inflict unconscious bias into the mix: for example good fielders will often be credited with more expected outs despite the data, and ballparks with high press boxes tend to score more line drives than ones with a lower press box.

Enter our Fielding Runs Above Average (FRAA). For most positions, FRAA is built from play-by-play data, which allows us to avoid the subjectivity found in many other fielding metrics. The idea is this: count how many fielding plays are made by a given player and compare that to expected plays for an average fielder at their position (based on pitcher ground ball tendencies and batter handedness). Then we adjust for park and base-out situations.

When it comes to catchers, our methodology is a little different thanks to the laundry list of responsibilities they're tasked with beyond just, well, catching and throwing the ball. By now you've probably heard about "framing" or the art of making umpires more likely to call balls outside the strike zone for strikes. To put this into one tidy number, we incorporate pitch tracking data (for the years it exists) and adjust for important factors like pitcher, umpire, batter and home-field advantage using a mixed-model approach. This grants us a number for how many strikes the catcher is personally adding to (or subtracting from) his pitchers' performance…which we then convert to runs added or lost using linear weights.

Framing is one of the biggest parts of determining catcher value, but we also take into account blocking balls from going past, whether a scorer deems it a passed ball or a wild pitch. We use a similar approach—one that really benefits from the pitch tracking data that tells us what ends up in the dirt and what doesn't. We also include a catcher's ability to prevent stolen bases and how well they field balls in play, and *finally* we come up with our FRAA for catchers.

Pitching

Both pitching and fielding make up the half of baseball that isn't run scoring: run prevention. Separating pitching from fielding is a tough task, and most recent pitching analysis has branched off from Voros McCracken's famous (and controversial) statement, "There is little if any difference among major-league pitchers in their ability to prevent hits on balls hit in the field of play." The research of the analytic community has validated this to some extent, and there are a host of "defense-independent" pitching measures that have been developed to try and extract the effect of the defense behind a hurler from the pitcher's work.

Our solution to this quandary is Deserved Run Average (DRA), our core pitching metric. DRA looks like earned run average (ERA), the tried-and-true pitching stat you've seen on every baseball broadcast or box score from the past century, but it's very different. To start, DRA takes an event-by-event look at what the pitchers does, and adjusts the value of that event based on different environmental factors like park, batter, catcher, umpire, base-out situation, run differential, inning, defense, home field advantage, pitcher role and temperature. That mixed model gives us a pitcher's expected contribution, similar to what we do for our DRC+ model for hitters and FRAA model for catchers. (Oh, and we also consider the pitcher's effect on basestealing and on balls getting past the catcher.)

It's important to note that DRA is set to the scale of runs allowed per nine innings (RA9) instead of ERA, which makes DRA's scale slightly higher than ERA's. The reason for this is because ERA tends to overrate three types of pitchers:

1. Pitchers who play in parks where scorers hand out more errors. Official scorers differ significantly in the frequency at which they assign errors to fielders.
2. Ground-ball pitchers, because a substantial proportion of errors occur on groundballs.
3. Pitchers who aren't very good. Better pitchers often allow fewer unearned runs than bad pitchers, because good pitchers tend to find ways to get out of jams.

Since the last time you picked up an edition of this book, we've also made a few minor changes to DRA to make it better. Recent research into "tunneling"—the act of throwing consecutive pitches that appear similar from a batter's point of view until after the swing decision point–data has given us a new contextual factor to account for in DRA: plate distance. This refers to the distance between successive pitches as they approach the plate, and while it has a smaller effect than factors like velocity or whiff rate, it still can help explain pitcher strikeout rate in our model.

New Pitching Metrics for 2020

We're including a few "new" pitching metrics in the book for the 2020 edition, though unlike last year, these numbers may be a little bit more familiar to those of you who have spent some time investigating baseball statistics.

Fastball Percentage

Our fastball percentage (FB%) statistic measures how frequently a pitcher throws a pitch classified as a "fastball," measured as a percentage of overall pitches thrown. We qualify three types of fastballs:

1. The traditional four-seam fastball;
2. The two-seam fastball or sinker;
3. "Hard cutters," which are pitches that have the movement profile of a cut fastball and are used as the pitcher's primary offering or in place of a more traditional fastball.

For example, a pitcher with a FB% of 67 throws any combination of these three pitches about two-thirds of the time.

Whiff Rate

Everybody loves a swing and a miss, and whiff rate (WHF) measures how frequently pitchers induce a swinging strike. To calculate WHF, we add up all the pitches thrown that ended with a swinging strike, then divide that number by a pitcher's total pitches thrown. Most often, high whiff rates correlate with high strikeout rates (and overall effective pitcher performance).

Called Strike Probability

Called Strike Probability (CSP) is a number that represents the likelihood that all of a pitcher's pitches will be called a strike while controlling for location, pitcher and batter handedness, umpire and count. Here's how it works: on each pitch, our model determines how many times (out of 100) that a similar pitch was called for a strike given those factors mentioned above, and when normalized for each batter's strike zone. Then we average the CSP for all pitches thrown by a pitcher in a season, and that gives us the yearly CSP percentage you see in the stats boxes.

As you might imagine, pitchers with a higher CSP are more likely to work in the zone, where pitchers with a lower CSP are likely locating their pitches outside the normal strike zone, for better or for worse.

Projections

Many of you aren't turning to this book just for a look at what a player has done, but for a look at what a player is going to do: the PECOTA projections. PECOTA, initially developed by Nate Silver (who has moved on to greater fame as a political analyst), consists of three parts:

1. Major-league equivalencies, which use minor-league statistics to project how a player will perform in the major leagues;
2. Baseline forecasts, which use weighted averages and regression to the mean to estimate a player's current true talent level; and
3. Aging curves, which uses the career paths of comparable players to estimate how a player's statistics are likely to change over time.

With all those important things covered, let's take a look at what's in the book this year.

Team Prospectus

Most of this book is composed of team chapters, with one for each of the 30 major-league franchises. On the first page of each chapter, you'll see a box that contains some of the key statistics for each team as well as a very inviting stadium diagram. (You can see an example of this for the Milwaukee Brewers on this very page!)

We start with the team name, their unadjusted 2019 win-loss record, and their divisional ranking. Beneath that are a host of other team statistics. **Pythag** presents an adjusted 2019 winning percentage, calculated by taking runs scored per game (**RS/G**) and runs allowed per game (**RA/G**) for the team, and running them through a version of Bill James' Pythagorean formula that was refined and improved by David Smyth and Brandon Heipp. (The formula is called "Pythagenpat," which is equally fun to type and to say.)

Next up is **DRC+**, described earlier, to indicate the overall hitting ability of the team either above or below league-average. Run prevention on the pitching side is covered by **DRA** (also mentioned earlier) and another metric: Fielding Independent Pitching (**FIP**), which calculates another ERA-like statistic based on strikeouts, walks, and home runs recorded. Defensive Efficiency Rating (**DER**) tells us the percentage of balls in play turned into outs for the team, and is a quick fielding shorthand that rounds out run prevention.

After that, we have several measures related to roster composition, as opposed to on-field performance. **B-Age** and **P-Age** tell us the average age of a team's batters and pitchers, respectively. **Salary** is the combined team payroll for all on-field players, and Doug Pappas' Marginal Dollars per Marginal Win (**M$/MW**) tells us how much money a team spent to earn production above replacement level.

Ending this batch of statistics is the number of disabled list days a team had over the season (**IL Days**) and the amount of salary paid to players on the disabled list (**$ on IL**); this final number is expressed as a percentage of total payroll.

Next to each of these stats, we've listed each team's MLB rank in that category from first to 30th. In this, first always indicates a positive outcome and 30th a negative outcome, except in the case of salary—first is highest.

After the franchise statistics, we share a few items about the team's home ballpark. There's the aforementioned diagram of the park's dimensions (including distances to the outfield wall), a graphic showing the height of the wall from the left-field pole to the right-field pole, and a table showing three-year park factors for the stadium. The park factors are displayed as indexes where 100 is average, 110 means that the park inflates the statistic in question by 10 percent, and 90 means that the park deflates the statistic in question by 10 percent.

On the second page of each team chapter, you'll find three graphs. The first is the **2019 Hit List Ranking**. This shows our Hit List Rank for the team on each day of the 2019 season and is intended to give you a picture of the ups and downs of the team's season. Hit List Rank measures overall team performance and drives the Hit List Power Rankings at the baseballprospectus.com website.

The second graph is **Committed Payroll** and helps you see how the team's payroll has compared to the MLB and divisional average payrolls over time. Payroll figures are current as of January 1, 2020; with so many free agents still unsigned as of this writing, the final 2020 figure will likely be significantly different for many teams. (In the meantime, you can always find the most current data at Baseball Prospectus' Cot's Baseball Contracts page.)

The third graph is **Farm System Ranking** and displays how the Baseball Prospectus prospect team has ranked the organization's farm system since 2007.

After the graphs, we have a **Personnel** section that lists many of the important decision-makers and upper-level field and operations staff members for the franchise, as well as any former Baseball Prospectus staff members who are currently part of the organization. (In very rare circumstances, someone might be on both lists!)

Juan Soto LF
Born: 10/25/98 Age: 21 Bats: L Throws: L
Height: 6'1" Weight: 185 Origin: International Free Agent, 2015

YEAR	TEAM	LVL	AGE	PA	R	2B	3B	HR	RBI	BB	K	SB	CS	AVG/OBP/SLG
2017	NAT	RK	18	27	3	1	1	0	4	2	1	0	0	.320/.370/.440
2017	HAG	A	18	96	15	5	0	3	14	10	8	1	2	.360/.427/.523
2018	HAG	A	19	74	12	5	3	5	24	14	13	2	0	.373/.486/.814
2018	POT	A+	19	73	17	3	1	7	18	11	8	0	1	.371/.466/.790
2018	HAR	AA	19	35	4	2	0	2	10	4	7	1	0	.323/.400/.581
2018	WAS	MLB	19	494	77	25	1	22	70	79	99	5	2	.292/.406/.517
2019	WAS	MLB	20	659	110	32	5	34	110	108	132	12	1	.282/.401/.548
2020	WAS	MLB	21	630	92	30	3	35	102	85	123	5	2	.284/.382/.543

Comparables: Ronald Acuña Jr., Mike Trout, Tony Conigliaro

YEAR	TEAM	LVL	AGE	PA	DRC+	VORP	BABIP	BRR	FRAA	WARP
2017	NAT	RK	18	27	135	1.5	.333	0.0	RF(9): -1.1	0.0
2017	HAG	A	18	96	181	8.0	.373	1.0	RF(19): -1.9, LF(2): -0.3	0.9
2018	HAG	A	19	74	222	14.5	.405	0.3	RF(14): 1.1, CF(2): 0.2	1.2
2018	POT	A+	19	73	260	15.4	.340	1.4	RF(14): 1.0, LF(1): 0.0	1.6
2018	HAR	AA	19	35	113	3.6	.364	0.0	LF(4): 0.6, RF(4): -0.5	0.1
2018	WAS	MLB	19	494	125	40.5	.338	-0.5	LF(114): 2.7	3.0
2019	WAS	MLB	20	659	136	49.0	.312	1.4	LF(150): -0.8	4.9
2020	WAS	MLB	21	630	133	43.6	.310	-0.1	LF 3	4.8

Position Players

After all that information and a thoughtful bylined essay covering each team, we present our player comments. These are also bylined, but due to frequent franchise shifts during the offseason, our bylines are more a rough guide than a perfect accounting of who wrote what.

Each player is listed with the major-league team that employed him as of early January 2020. If a player changed teams after that point via free agency, trade, or any other method, you'll be able to find them in the chapter for their previous squad.

As an example, take a look at the player comment for Nationals outfielder Juan Soto: the stat block that accompanies his written comment is at the top of this page. First we cover biographical information (age is as of June 30, 2020) before moving onto the stats themselves. Our statistic columns include standard identifying information like **YEAR**, **TEAM**, **LVL** (level of affiliated play) and **AGE** before getting into the numbers. Next, we provide raw, untranslated numbers like you might find on the back of your dad's baseball cards: **PA** (plate appearances), **R** (runs), **2B** (doubles), **3B** (triples), **HR** (home runs), **RBI** (runs batted in), **BB** (walks), **K** (strikeouts), **SB** (stolen bases) and **CS** (caught stealing).

Next, we have unadjusted "slash" statistics: **AVG** (batting average), **OBP** (on-base percentage) and **SLG** (slugging percentage). Following the slash line is **DRC+** (Deserved Runs Created Plus), which we described earlier as total offensive expected contribution compared to the league average.

One of our oldest active metrics, **VORP** (Value Over Replacement Player), considers offensive production, position and plate appearances. In essence, it is the number of runs contributed beyond what a replacement-level player at the same position would contribute if given the same percentage of team plate appearances. VORP does not consider the quality of a player's defense.

BABIP (batting average on balls in play) tells us how often a ball in play fell for a hit, and can help us identify whether a batter may have been lucky or not…but note that high BABIPs also tend to follow the great hitters of our time, as well as speedy singles hitters who put the ball on the ground.

The next item is **BRR** (Baserunning Runs), which covers all of a player's baserunning accomplishments including (but not limited to) swiped bags and failed attempts. Next is **FRAA** (Fielding Runs Above Average), which also includes the number of games previously played at each position noted in parentheses. Multi-position players have only their two most frequent positions listed here, but their total FRAA number reflects all positions played.

Our last column here is **WARP** (Wins Above Replacement Player). WARP estimates the total value of a player, which means for hitters it takes into account hitting runs above average (calculated using the DRC+ model), BRR and FRAA. Then, it makes an adjustment for positions played and gives the player a credit for plate appearances based upon the difference between "replacement level"—which is derived from the quality of players added to a team's roster after the start of the season–and the league average.

The final line just below the stats box is **PECOTA** data, which is discussed further in a following section.

Catchers

Catchers are a special breed, and thus they have earned their own separate box which displays some of the defensive metrics that we've built just for them. As an example, let's check out J.T. Realmuto.

The **YEAR** and **TEAM** columns match what you'd find in the other stat box. **P. COUNT** indicates the number of pitches thrown while the catcher was behind the plate, including swinging strikes, fouls and balls in play. **FRM RUNS** is the total run value the catcher provided (or cost) his team by influencing the umpire to call strikes where other catchers did not. **BLK RUNS** expresses the total run value above or below average for the catcher's ability to prevent wild pitches and passed balls. **THRW RUNS** is calculated using a similar model as the previous two statistics, and it measures a catcher's ability to throw out basestealers but also to dissuade them from testing his arm in the first place. It takes into account factors like the pitcher (including his delivery and pickoff move) and baserunner (who could be as fast as Billy Hamilton or as slow as Yonder Alonso). **TOT RUNS** is the sum of all of the previous three statistics.

Justin Verlander RHP
Born: 02/20/83   Age: 37   Bats: R   Throws: R
Height: 6'5"   Weight: 225   Origin: Round 1, 2004 Draft (#2 overall)

YEAR	TEAM	LVL	AGE	W	L	SV	G	GS	IP	H	HR	BB/9	K/9	K	GB%	BABIP
2017	DET	MLB	34	10	8	0	28	28	172	153	23	3.5	9.2	176	34%	.283
2017	HOU	MLB	34	5	0	0	5	5	34	17	4	1.3	11.4	43	32%	.194
2018	HOU	MLB	35	16	9	0	34	34	214	156	28	1.6	12.2	290	31%	.272
2019	HOU	MLB	36	21	6	0	34	34	223	137	36	1.7	12.1	300	36%	.219
2020	HOU	MLB	37	15	6	0	29	29	184	138	28	2.3	12.1	248	35%	.274

Comparables: Zack Greinke, A.J. Burnett, Aníbal Sánchez

YEAR	TEAM	LVL	AGE	WHIP	ERA	DRA	WARP	MPH	FB%	WHF	CSP
2017	DET	MLB	34	1.28	3.82	4.03	3.0	97.7	58	11	47.8
2017	HOU	MLB	34	0.65	1.06	3.08	0.9	97.5	59.6	15.1	49.9
2018	HOU	MLB	35	0.90	2.52	2.33	7.3	97.5	61.2	16.2	51.6
2019	HOU	MLB	36	0.80	2.58	2.51	7.9	96.8	49.9	17.5	48.3
2020	HOU	MLB	37	1.01	2.75	2.95	5.3	95.8	54.6	15.1	48.2

Pitchers

Let's give our pitchers a turn, using 2019 AL Cy Young winner Justin Verlander as our example. Take a look at his stat block: the first line and the **YEAR**, **TEAM**, **LVL** and **AGE** columns are the same as in the position player example earlier.

Here too, we have a series of columns that display raw, unadjusted statistics compiled by the pitcher over the course of a season: **W** (wins), **L** (losses), **SV** (saves), **G** (games pitched), **GS** (games started), **IP** (innings pitched), **H** (hits allowed) and **HR** (home runs allowed). Next we have two statistics that are rates: **BB/9** (walks per nine innings) and **K/9** (strikeouts per nine innings), before returning to the unadjusted K (strikeouts).

Next up is **GB%** (ground ball percentage), which is the percentage of all batted balls that were hit on the ground, including both outs and hits. Remember, this is based on observational data and subject to human error, so please approach this with a healthy dose of skepticism.

BABIP (batting average on balls in play) is calculated using the same methodology as it is for position players, but it often tells us more about a pitcher than it does a hitter. With pitchers, a high BABIP is often due to poor defense or bad luck, and can often be an indicator of potential rebound, and a low BABIP may be cause to expect performance regression. (A typical league-average BABIP is close to .290-.300.)

The metrics **WHIP** (walks plus hits per inning pitched) and **ERA** (earned run average) are old standbys: WHIP measures walks and hits allowed on a per-inning basis, while ERA measures earned runs on a nine-inning basis. Neither of these stats are translated or adjusted.

DRA (Deserved Run Average) was described at length earlier, and measures how many runs the pitcher "deserved" to allow per nine innings. Please note that since we lack all the data points that would make for a "real" DRA for minor-league events, the DRA displayed for minor league partial-seasons is based off of different data. (That data is a modified version of our cFIP metric, which you can find more information about on our website.)

Just like with hitters, **WARP** (Wins Above Replacement Player) is a total value metric that puts pitchers of all stripes on the same scale as position players. We use DRA as the primary input for our calculation of WARP. You might notice that relief pitchers (due to their limited innings) may have a lower WARP than you were expecting or than you might see in other WARP-like metrics. WARP does not take leverage into account, just the actions a pitcher performs and the expected value of those actions...which ends up judging high-leverage relief pitchers differently than you might imagine given their prestige and market value.

MPH gives you the pitcher's 95th percentile velocity for the noted season, in order to give you an idea of what the *peak* fastball velocity a pitcher possesses. Since this comes from our pitch-tracking data, it is not publicly available for minor-league pitchers.

Finally, we display the three new pitching metrics we described earlier. **FB%** (fastball percentage) gives you the percentage of fastballs thrown out of all pitches. **WHF** (whiff rate) tells you the percentage of swinging strikes induced out of all pitches. **CSP** (called strike probability) expresses the likelihood of all pitches thrown to result in a called strike, after controlling for factors like handedness, umpire, pitch type, count and location.

PECOTA

All players have PECOTA projections for 2020, as well as a set of other numbers that describe the performance of comparable players according to PECOTA. All projections for 2020 are for the player at the date we went to press in early January and are projected into the league and park context as indicated by the team abbreviation. (Note that players at very low levels of the minors are too unpredictable to assess using these numbers.) All PECOTA projected statistics represent a player's projected major-league performance.

Below the projections are the player's three highest-scoring comparable players as determined by PECOTA. All comparables represent a snapshot of how the listed player was performing at the same age as the current player, so if a

23-year-old pitcher is compared to Bartolo Colón, he's actually being compared to a 23-year-old Colón, not the version that pitched for the Rangers in 2018, nor to Colón's career as a whole.

A few points about pitcher projections. First, we aren't yet projecting peak velocity, so that column will be blank in the PECOTA lines. Second, projecting DRA is trickier than evaluating past performance, because it is unclear how deserving each pitcher will be of his anticipated outcomes. However, we know that another DRA-related statistic–contextual FIP or cFIP–estimates future run scoring very well. So for PECOTA, the projected DRA figures you see are based on the past cFIPs generated by the pitcher and comparable players over time, along with the other factors described above.

Lineouts

In each chapter's Lineouts section, you'll find abbreviated text comments, as well as all the same information you'd find in our full player comments. The only difference is that we limit the stats boxes in this section to only including the 2019 information for each player.

Managers

After all those wonderful team chapters, we've got statistics for each big-league manager, all of whom are organized by alphabetical order. Here you'll find a block including an extraordinary amount of information collected from each manager's entire career. For more information on the acronyms and what they mean, please visit the Glossary at www.baseballprospectus.com.

There is one important metric that we'd like to call attention to, and you'll find it next to each manager's name: **wRM+** (weighted reliever management plus). Developed by Rob Arthur and Rian Watt, wRM+ investigates how good a manager is at using their best relievers during the moments of highest leverage, using both our proprietary DRA metric as well as Leverage Index. wRM+ is scaled to a league average of 100, and a wRM+ of 105 indicates that relievers were used approximately five percent "better" than average. On the other hand, a wRM+ of 95 would tell us the team used its relievers five percent "worse" than the average team.

While wRM+ does not have an extremely strong correlation with a manager, it is statistically significant; this means that a manager is not *entirely* responsible for a team's wRM+, but does have some effect on that number.

PECOTA Leaderboards

If you're familiar with PECOTA, then you'll have noticed that the projection system often appears bullish on players coming off a bad year and bearish on players coming off a good year. (This is because the system weights several previous seasons, not just the most recent one.) In addition, we publish the 50th

Philadelphia Phillies 2020

percentile projections for each player–which is smack in the middle of the range of projected production—which tends to mean PECOTA stat lines don't often have extreme results like 40 home runs or 250 strikeouts in a given season. In essence, PECOTA doesn't project very many extreme seasons.

At the end of the book, we've ranked the top players at each position based on their PECOTA projections. This might help you visualize just how a given player's projection compares to that of their peers, so that even if a dramatic stat line isn't projected, you can still imagine how they stack up against the rest of the league.

Part 1: Team Analysis

Philadelphia Phillies: Where Are You Going, Where Have You Been?

Justin Klugh, Jarrett Seidler and Matthew Trueblood

2019: What Went Right
The rightness of the 2019 Phillies season starts and ends with Andrew McCutchen wearing the team's infamous Saturday Night Special alternate uniforms. These uniforms have been universally reviled since the Carter administration, but Cutch made it work in a way fashion scientists are still trying to understand. You can try to explain to me that other things went right in a realer way for the Phillies this season. You will fail.

PECOTA had predicted the Phillies to win 86 games in what was supposed to be a competitive NL East, but you didn't need an advanced projection system to know this team was aiming high. You just needed the image of principal owner John Middleton and super-agent Scott Boras hugging like they were, as one fan accurately put it, "drunk at prom" in the background of footage featuring the team's $330 million free agent signee, Bryce Harper. No metric was going to convince people watching the Phillies bring in a superstar like Harper—among other big improvements—that they had an 86-win ceiling.

Before chaos reared its many heads, Matt Klentak and his front office executed their plan to sign the closest thing to sure things in McCutchen and David Robertson. Both had healthy track records, and along with trades for Jean Segura and J.T. Realmuto, the Phillies addressed areas of need and simultaneously solved overpopulation issues while giving away nothing they couldn't afford.

The only exception to this might have been the Phillies' top prospect, pitcher Sixto Sánchez, who was dealt to Miami for Realmuto. However, once Realmuto got rolling, it was difficult not to see the appeal in having the best catcher in baseball on your team to hit .275 with 25 home runs and a team-leading 5.6 WARP while catching a league-leading 47 percent of runners.

Realmuto wasn't the only boon of the offseason, either. Before a ghost bit the ACL in his left knee, McCutchen's .378 OBP was the second highest among Phillies starters, and his .834 OPS was third. From Opening Day to June 3, he had the third highest WAR on the team (1.5) and the second highest walk rate (16.4 percent) in 262 plate appearances from the leadoff spot. The subtraction of McCutchen from the batting order sent a demoralizing ripple effect through this team from which it never recovered.

Scott Kingery missed time with a right hamstring strain, but (arbitrary endpoints ahoy) from May 19 to June 30, he slashed .292/.342/.556, undergoing significant improvements in each category, most notably slugging. The Phillies have been anxious to rely on Kingery's versatility since giving him a six-year contract extension before he'd played an inning of big-league ball, and though he tapered off in a big way (his .230/.292/.418 second half included a hard fall in September), his steps forward were very real. On a better, more consistent team, Kingery would have been the everyday role-player who, in Zobrist-ian fashion, bridged the wounds that take regulars out of the lineup and give at-bats to replacement-level players and that may yet be his best role in the future.

The Phillies' top draft pick in 2017, outfielder Adam Haseley, was forced into service due to injuries and gave the team a legitimate center fielder. He was deployed to all fields and made multiple diving catches in every one of them while providing some pop at the plate. Along with Bryce Harper's improved defense, the 23-year-old Haseley gave the Phillies a few ways to find outs in the outfield.

You may have noticed these claims of "rightness" are rather segmented, which is pretty much how this team cobbled together its form of contention. The Phillies spent 60 days alone in first place in the NL East, but never visited after June 9. They sank as low as fourth place later in the season, clinging to a potential Wild Card berth by their teeth thanks in large part to the NL's paltry competitive offerings. Their lineup of talented hitters could not seem to get hot at the same time: Rhys Hoskins handled April (.279 BA, 1.001 OPS, 8 HR), Cesar Hernandez took May (.327 BA, .931 OPS, 8 2B), Kingery was on fire in May and June when he wasn't hurt, Segura started seeing the ball around July (.346 BA, .814 OPS in 82 PA), and Realmuto (.295 BA, .935 OPS, 6 HR, 11 2B) went off in August. Brad Miller hit eight home runs (.800 SLG) in 55 September at-bats.

And then, there was Harper. Or in some cases, there wasn't. Dragging the expectations of a $330 million price-tag behind him, Harper would have had a hard time producing results deemed "acceptable" below an MVP season, and he did not have one of those. He slashed .260/.372/.510 with 35 home runs, 114 RBI and a 14.5-percent walk rate. A good season, and actually one of his best. He picked up steam as the season went on, hitting .277/.372/.598 down the stretch, and flashed the defensive prowess that had been dormant in 2018. Nevertheless, it was clear he couldn't carry the team himself.

Klentak showed an aptitude for picking up position players on the fly; Jay Bruce paid immediate dividends before fading away and Corey Dickerson became one of the team's biggest threats, hitting .293, with more than half of his 39 hits being for extra bases from August to mid-September when a broken foot ended his season.

2019: What Went Wrong

To illustrate why this team cracked and eventually split, it's best to start in the middle. The trade deadline was illustrative of everything that was already wrong with them on the field and questionable about them organizationally. Then, when they actually made some deals, it started further debate about what they had done—and more notably, not done—and what that said about their own confidence in the team they'd built.

Losing McCutchen in June broke the Phillies. He wasn't their best hitter or their best fielder, but losing him for the season seemed to ignite a series of unsolvable problems. This is largely due to the fact that you can't solve chaos. The Phillies tried to, of course. As stated earlier, Klentak brought in McCutchen and setup man Robertson because of their consistent health histories. Collectively, they played in 59 games for the Phillies in 2019. Robertson appeared in zero of them.

Robertson, however, was just the tip of the bullpen's imploding iceberg. Seranthony Domínguez, the Phillies closer of the future, suffered from pain in his elbow and pitched only 24 2/3 innings. Victor Arano was expected to be a key figure in the Phillies 'pen, as well; he appeared in three games before undergoing arthroscopic surgery. Edubray Ramos had bicep tendonitis, missed most of the season, came back in September, and in the first pitch of his glorious return, gave up a home run to Franmil Reyes. Adam Morgan, Tommy Hunter, Pat Neshek: One by one, the Phillies relievers were taken from them, forcing them to resort to scrap-heap come leavings like Blake Parker, Jared Hughes, and Mike Morin, who collectively contributed 0.9 WARP in 76 innings.

Despite the shuffling, the bullpen had been aggressively average; while not the worst, it was far from the strength the Phillies believed they had started the season with, intending for their relievers and their offense to prop up a shallow rotation. The only part of that plan that came to fruition was the part in which the rotation was a weakness. Jake Arrieta attempted to pitch through some bone spurs, but the bone spurs won. As part of an ongoing narrative in which pitchers questioned the philosophies of the Phillies' pitching development and coaching staff, in mid-August, Zach Eflin diverted from the game plan they'd set up for him and, as a former sinkerballer, went back to sinkerballing. He saw a lot of success after an absolutely miserable stretch from July 4 to August 10 in which he logged an ERA of 9.70 through eight starts, featuring fun little tidbits like 4.2 walks per nine and 2.5 home runs per nine From August 17 on, however, he and his sinker had a 3.20 ERA, 14 walks, and 30 strikeouts in 45 innings. Nick Pivetta, projected to have a breakout year, broke the other way and was in the bullpen at season's end. Vince Velasquez was briefly relegated to the 'pen only to return to the rotation, still repeatedly undone by throwing a lot of pitches to get only a couple of outs.

Aaron Nola was the No. 1 starter and recipient of the bona fide ace tag after accumulating 6.6 WARP in 212 1/3 innings in 2018, but his 4.89 ERA and 4.0 walks per nine through June 15 left the Phillies at a loss. Nola eventually found his stuff, but he fell off again in September and the Phillies lost all of his final seven starts—during that span his ERA was 5.27.

The Phillies needed to add starting pitching. They had pursued Patrick Corbin in the offseason but couldn't land him. There had been others available: J.A. Happ. Wade Miley. Charlie Morton. The Phillies acquired none of them. They stayed away from Dallas Keuchel entirely. After experiencing the full power of a rotation that in the first half accumulated a collective 4.56 ERA (14th in the NL), 1.72 HR/9 (15th in the NL), and 18.5 percent HR/FB rate (13th in the NL), it was clear they'd bet on the wrong pitchers.

The Phillies poked around a bit, and discovered they were knee-deep in a stagnant pitching market, unable to really improve without giving too much away—and improve to do what, exactly? Ken Rosenthal characterized the Phillies at the trade deadline as being so wary of the NL's best teams that "going for it" only to get a Wild Card spot wouldn't be worth what they'd have to give up for the available upgrades. Tanner Roark, the Reds reportedly told them, would have cost them 2016 No. 1 overall draft pick Mickey Moniak. In addition, the drop-off between top targets and lesser targets was quite spacious. Instead of putting together a trade for Madison Bumgarner or Mike Minor, the team dealt for Jason Vargas, who had been glowering at people from the bottom of the Mets' rotation, and signed Drew Smyly, who had been chewing on a corn cob out by the trash. This went about as well as you'd expect, and the Phillies failed to find the consistency that had eluded them for the entirety of the season's first half. The failure to bail out the pitching staff put a lot of pressure on the offense, which churned out pedestrian team numbers, even with the occasional flare-ups of individual players. In most offensive categories, they were just below average.

And then there was the manager. To some, Gabe Kapler was the sole destroyer of the 2019 season. This cannot possibly be true, though he continued to be responsible for befuddling in-game decisions, perplexing bullpen management, and attempts at galaxy-brained matchups. But every decision—every Sean Rodriguez start, every pitching change that should have been a double switch, every pitcher sent in to pinch-run for another pitcher—can be melted down to a statistic Kapler saw as an advantage. Going with your gut isn't a sure thing, but a blind fealty to the numbers is an abdication that avoids the hard work of judgment.

That said, Kapler was merely the in-game presence of the Phillies front office, which from a player-evaluation standpoint raised a lot of flags about itself over the course of a second consecutive season somehow defined by deflation, half-measures, and steps in the wrong direction—this despite the acquisition of one of the most famous baseball players in the world and the best catcher in the sport. —*Justin Klugh*

Prospect Outlook

Despite key trades and graduations, the cupboard still isn't quite bare. The Phillies took Wichita State third baseman **Alec Bohm** third overall in 2018, and he made it up to Double-A for the second half of his first full season. He's a very well-rounded hitting prospect with substantial raw power that he's still working on converting fully into games. He's not likely to ever surpass fringy-ness at third base, but this is a franchise that played Maikel Franco at the hot corner 600 times since 2014. He'll be a 2020 roster contender pretty early on in the season at a position where the Phillies sorely need the help.

Pitcher **Spencer Howard** could've been up this season if he hadn't missed more than two months with shoulder fatigue. Even then, he still might've made it as an impact 'pen arm if the Phillies were truer contenders. Howard followed through on his late-season 2018 emergence by dominating the Advanced-A and Double-A levels with a fastball that comfortably reaches the upper-90s complemented by a full four-pitch mix. He'll be pretty firmly in the 2020 big-league mix as well.

Howard's stock crossed with **Adonis Medina's** over the course of the season. Medina was our 57th-ranked prospect entering the year and battled the cozy confines of Reading to something of a draw. He's never really made the gains or even consolidations that we've been projecting onto him for some time. His fastball isn't always sufficiently explosive, and he's never found a consistent breaking ball. The bullpen looms as a possibility.

The rest of the Phillies system is buoyed by low-level fliers and former low-level fliers who now form an interesting group of upper-minors pitching depth. The best of the A-ball arms is power pitcher **Francisco Morales**, who started to gel by the end of the Low-A season, and could move at a Howard-like pace next year if things go well. The bats are led by 2019 first-rounder **Bryson Stott**, who could move quickly himself. In the high-minors, the Phillies have plenty of close-to-the-majors arms to choose from, including lefty starter **JoJo Romero**, rising sleeper **Damon Jones**, and big relief arm **Kyle Dohy**.

We'd be remiss if we didn't mention 2016 1.1 draft pick **Mickey Moniak**. He had a superficially improved power season at Reading, but still hasn't regained the sheen or projection of a top overall pick. He's getting close to the majors and the package will still play as is, just not at an impact level. —*Jarrett Seidler*

Philadelphia Phillies 2020

2020 Outlook

In the winter of 2018-19, the Phillies were the team that lurked forever, tinkering, and then made a massive splash near the start of spring training, signing Harper and trading for Realmuto. This year, they made most of their news at the front end of the offseason. Firing Gabe Kapler felt like an ownership-dictated rebuke of the team's attempts to go hypermodern, and if there had been any lingering doubts to that effect, hiring Joe Girardi in Kapler's stead surely wiped them out. Girardi's openness to advanced information wasn't at issue when the Yankees moved on from him; it was more about his old-fashioned style of communicating with both the front office and the clubhouse. That style now migrates to Philadelphia, where it will certainly charm a large segment of the fan base in the near term, and where the dynamics above the field level might be more conducive to it.

Lest anyone worry that John Middleton had been all talk when he said the Harper deal would only engender more spending, the Phillies handed out the first nine-figure pact of the winter, signing Zack Wheeler for five years. Wheeler is an interesting way for the team to lay down its chips since so much of his perceived upside lies in the measurable and markedly sabermetric things the team otherwise seemed to deviate from. Nonetheless, he slides into the No. 2 slot in their projected rotation and could help it be much more consistent in 2020.

Didi Gregorius is an even more interesting fit, though an easier one to explain. Signing Gregorius gave the Phillies the chance to slide Jean Segura back to second base, where he's a better fit defensively. It also provided balance to a lineup that leaned right, especially in its lower half. There's also a pre-existing relationship between Gregorius and Girardi. Still, he's a player who hasn't yet bounced back from a severe injury, and whose skill set suggests he might not age all that well.

After those moves, Klentak stayed on the edges, only making very small moves. Josh Harrison and Nick Martini deepen the bench, but don't offer much upside. Martini's arrival also made it easier for the team to move on from Odubel Herrera—an admirable goal—after Herrera transgressed Major League Baseball's (and humanity's) domestic violence policy. Harrison helps make up for the lost infield depth stemming from the team's decision to let both Franco and Cesar Hernandez go via non-tender. Francisco Liriano gives the team another decent left-handed option out of the bullpen, but he's a platoon-vulnerable hurler at this stage, so the three-batter minimum might make life difficult for him.

The Phillies' depth is fine, though far from inspiring. The signature characteristic of this team, though, is the high variance in possible production from their headliners. Harper, Hoskins, Realmuto, McCutchen, Gregorius, Nola, Wheeler, and Arrieta have the ability to perform so well that the rest of the roster only needs to avoid being a black hole, but they each also have significant risk, even in the short term. Their moves this winter did nothing to change that risk profile. —*Matthew Trueblood*

Performance Graphs

2019 Hit List Ranking

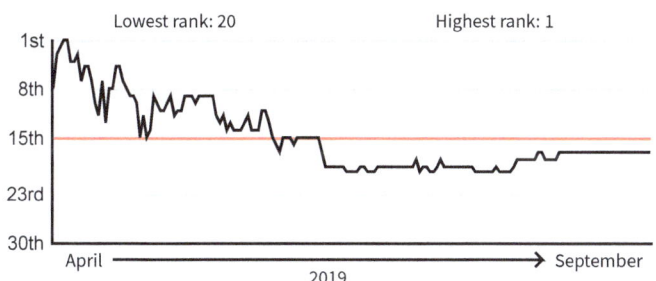

Committed Payroll (in millions)

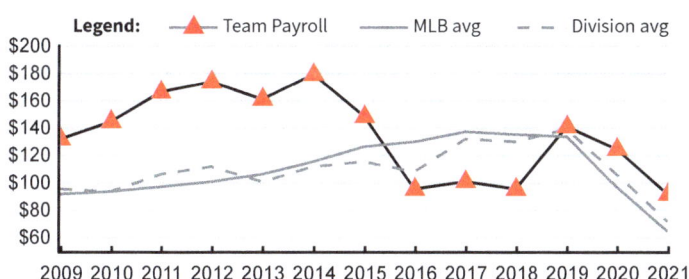

Farm System Ranking

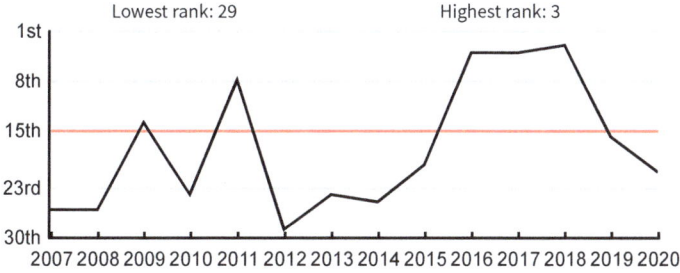

2019 Team Performance

ACTUAL STANDINGS

Team	W	L	Pct
ATL	97	65	0.599
WAS	93	69	0.574
NYN	86	76	0.531
PHI	**81**	**81**	**0.500**
MIA	57	105	0.352

THIRD-ORDER STANDINGS

Team	W	L	Pct
WAS	95	67	0.584
ATL	89	73	0.550
NYN	88	74	0.542
PHI	**74**	**88**	**0.457**
MIA	60	102	0.373

TOP HITTERS

Player	WARP
J.T. Realmuto	5.6
Bryce Harper	3.7
Rhys Hoskins	2.4

TOP PITCHERS

Player	WARP
Aaron Nola	5.1
Héctor Neris	1.8
Zach Eflin	1.1

VITAL STATISTICS

Statistic Name	Value	Rank
Pythagenpat	.488	17th
Runs Scored per Game	4.78	14th
Runs Allowed per Game	4.90	18th
Deserved Runs Created Plus	90	22nd
Deserved Run Average	4.93	17th
Fielding Independent Pitching	4.83	20th
Defensive Efficiency Rating	.702	17th
Batter Age	27.5	7th
Pitcher Age	28.1	16th
Salary	$140.6M	13th
Marginal $ per Marginal Win	$3.9M	14th
Injured List Days	1418	24th
$ on IL	27%	26th

2020 Team Projections

PROJECTED STANDINGS

Team	W	L	Pct	+/-
NYN	87.8	74.2	0.542	2
WAS	87.1	74.9	0.538	-6
ATL	82.8	79.2	0.511	-14
PHI	**76.8**	**85.2**	**0.474**	**-4**
MIA	71.3	90.7	0.440	14

TOP PROJECTED HITTERS

Player	WARP
J.T. Realmuto	4.2
Rhys Hoskins	2.8
Bryce Harper	2.8

TOP PROJECTED PITCHERS

Player	WARP
Aaron Nola	3.7
Zack Wheeler	2.4
Vince Velasquez	0.9

FARM SYSTEM REPORT

Top Prospect	Number of Top 101 Prospects
Spencer Howard, #36	2

KEY DEDUCTIONS

Player	WARP
César Hernández	1.8
Corey Dickerson	1.4
Brad Miller	0.9
Maikel Franco	0.3
Drew Smyly	0.2
Nick Vincent	0.2
Logan Morrison	0.0
Edubray Ramos	0.0
Jerad Eickhoff	-0.1
Juan Nicasio	-0.1

KEY ADDITIONS

Player	WARP
Zack Wheeler	2.4
Didi Gregorius	1.6
Odúbel Herrera	0.7
Alec Bohm	0.6
Damon Jones	0.3
T.J. Rivera	0.2
JoJo Romero	0.2
Logan Forsythe	0.1
Nick Martini	0.1
Neil Walker	0.0

Team Personnel

President
Andy MacPhail

Vice President & General Manager
Matt Klentak

Assistant General Manager
Brian Minniti

Assistant General Manager
Scott Proefrock

Assistant General Manager
Ned Rice

Manager
Joe Girardi

BP Alumni
Lewie Pollis
Alex Rosen

Citizens Bank Park Stats

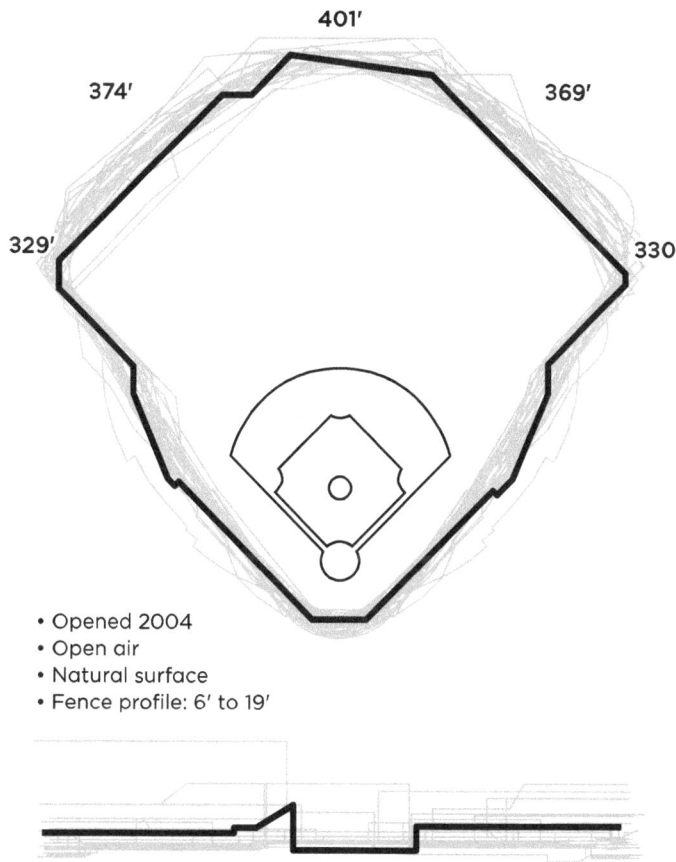

- Opened 2004
- Open air
- Natural surface
- Fence profile: 6' to 19'

Three-Year Park Factors

Runs	Runs/RH	Runs/LH	HR/RH	HR/LH
103	104	99	113	110

Phillies Team Analysis

Most everyone who might be reading this is familiar with the story of Romeo and Juliet, if not through a required high school reading of William Shakespeare's play, then through the sprawling net of imaginings and re-imaginings that have been cast over the past 400 years. Everyone knows it's a tragedy—the very prologue of the play announces it:

> From forth the fatal loins of these two foes
> A pair of star-cross'd lovers take their life;
> Whose misadventured piteous overthrows
> Do with their death bury their parents' strife. (I.i.5-8)[1]

To call a baseball season—any season, no matter how bad—a tragedy makes no sense, not in the context of the wide world in which we live. A baseball season is a tally of won games and lost games, that's all. Those wins and losses break hearts, sure. But a tragedy in the more common, less theatrical definition of the word? No. And yet, here is "Romeo and Juliet" in the Phillies essay, or rather *Romeo + Juliet*, Baz Luhrmann's garish, extravagant 1996 tumble through Shakespeare's text, and that is because *Romeo + Juliet* is a baseball movie.

In Luhrmann's iteration, Romeo's banishment from Verona for killing Juliet's cousin Tybalt takes Romeo to a dust-swept RV park, and as bad news speeds toward him and good news blows away on a missed package notice come unstuck from his door, Romeo stands out back, hitting stones with a bat made of a broken branch. As far as baseball film tropes go, the image is iconic, even though it's anguish and rage and probably boredom that toss the stone up and crank the stick forward in this iteration, not the yard-bound dreams of youth. Romeo has a whole bucket of stones, but the viewer only watches him hit one. It sounds like he makes good contact.

⚾   ⚾   ⚾

The ending of "Romeo and Juliet" is so wrenching because it almost works out. With Friar Lawrence's help, Juliet fakes death to escape another marriage and is given a perfect hiding place in the Capulet vault to wait for Romeo and their future together. If Romeo gets the right message, sleeping Juliet can be spirited from the tomb and the two young lovers have the promise of happily ever after. But Romeo gets only the message of the appearance—Juliet's death—and he goes to the tomb bearing poison. He kills himself a moment before Juliet wakes, and she, in despair, takes up his dagger. Many stagings of the play toy with the nearness of the miss: Juliet's hand moves while Romeo looks elsewhere or the actor gives some other signal that happiness could be mere seconds away, until it isn't. Luhrmann's iteration of the scene is so striking because they're both conscious at the same time. A poisoned Romeo watches Juliet wake. They speak their last lines to each other, not to the dark air of the tomb, and it's still too late. By seconds, by a knife's edge, still too late.

The 2019 Phillies season did not come down to any kind of tenterhooked almost. Instead, the 2019 Phillies enacted their slow-motion collapse as Atlanta and, more meteorically, Washington, climbed. But the Phillies might have been chasing real success. If the admittedly thin rotation had performed at least to expectation—if Aaron Nola hadn't opened and closed the year with uncharacteristic hittableness; if Jake Arrieta's elbow hadn't developed another bone spur. If the front office had done more to bolster pitching altogether; if the one splashy offseason bullpen addition—David Robertson—hadn't found himself hurt and in Dr. James Andrews's office and facing more than the loss of one season. If Andrew McCutchen hadn't been waylaid by a knee injury a mere third of the way through. If Rhys Hoskins hadn't fallen into a slump so deep it might have been a grave. If Pat Neshek, if Tommy Hunter—

How many *ifs* can one narrative sustain?

If, in Shakespeare's play, the messenger hadn't been obstructed by plague quarantine. If, in Luhrmann's film, the package delivery notice hadn't blown away. If, in all versions, Romeo had arrived five minutes later. If only.

⚾ ⚾ ⚾

Though what most remember of Romeo's friend Mercutio in *Romeo + Juliet* is Harold Perrineau in a glittering silver skirt and crimson lipstick passing out ecstasy, all iterations of Mercutio attempt to bring reason to the play. Mercutio, as neither Montague nor Capulet, feels no reflexive obligation toward the central blood feud. Mercutio is playful where others are serious, which is to say, Mercutio treats the cycle of insult and honor as only so much puffery. Though the play doesn't openly acknowledge as much, an ounce of the same attitude from both the warring families would make this a comedy, not a tragedy. Instead, the play forces Mercutio's hand and pulls him into the violence, too. As he's dying, fatally wounded in an attempt to protect Romeo from Juliet's cousin Tybalt, he curses the Capulets and the Montagues for both houses' inability to see sense and make peace.

Earlier in the play, Mercutio even questions Romeo's impulsive, youthful passions (which are the same passions that lead to a double suicide at the story's close). Mercutio does this in the famous Queen Mab speech, in which the fairies' midwife manipulates dreams and makes mischief. This speech is often presented as sheer fancy (in Luhrmann's film, Mercutio is literally on drugs at the time), but in context, it serves as a reality check. Mercutio uses whimsy to mock Romeo's hyperbolic, melancholic mooning over Rosaline, the girl for whom Romeo is sick with love at the play's opening and the girl for whom Romeo spares not a thought the moment he sees Juliet. Mercutio derides the extremity of Romeo's sentiment, and, when Romeo begins to convey what is sure to be a melodramatic portent, Mercutio, sagely, has no patience for it:

> ROMEO
> I dreamt a dream tonight.
> MERCUTIO
> And so did I.
> ROMEO
> Well, what was yours?
> MERCUTIO
> That dreamers often lie. (I.iv.53-56)[2]

Later in the same scene, while Romeo protests the veracity of his feelings (which are soon to be revealed as easily dismissed), Mercutio says,

> True, I talk of dreams,
> Which are the children of an idle brain,
> Begot of nothing but vain fantasy,
> Which is as thin of substance as the air. (I.iv.103-106)[3]

See reason, Mercutio says. But reason isn't romantic. Pragmatism doesn't sell tissues or tickets, and pragmatism flew out the window on Thursday, August 15, when, with the bases loaded, in the bottom of the ninth, Bryce Harper muscled Derek Holland's 2-2 sinker hand over hand into the second deck for the single most satisfying moment of the season. There's your balcony scene, Philadelphia. But you know how this play ends. Don't get your hopes up when Juliet's eyelids flutter.

⚾   ⚾   ⚾

It's the contemplation of what might have been that is so wrenching, the heady heights of the early acts. The team spent sixty spring days in first place in the NL East, but a terrible conclusion to June—one marked by a centerpiece of a seven-game skid—kicked into motion that steady decline. Though it would take until September's six-game losing streak to echo June's particular awfulness, the more damning piece was that the Phillies couldn't conjure success on a similar scale, not once all season. The team enjoyed a handful of four-game win streaks over the course of the season, but only one of those came in the second half. They did not find a way to "go on a tear." What they found was a way to infuriatingly replicate too many of the worst parts of 2018, despite real and reasonable improvements in the offseason. The 2019 Phillies roster was significantly, objectively better than 2018's, and yet the tangible effects of that improvement equaled one additional win.

Definitions of tragedy, in their theatrical or literary sense, generally hinge on the question of hamartia, which most take to signify the protagonist's fatal flaw. The source of the flaw in this sense is within the character's control: it's an excess of pride, ambition, indecision, suggestibility, jealousy. The literary world has a tragedy for every season, and it's easy enough to map any of those onto baseball and to add a few more: miserliness, naivete, moral bankruptcy. But what if it's not so easy to point a specific finger? (Or what if there are simply too many things at which to point?)

Scholar Jules Brody offers an older definition of the word:

> Hamartia is a morally neutral non-normative term, derived from the verb hamartano, meaning "to miss the mark," "to fall short of an objective." And by extension: to reach one destination rather than the intended one; to make a mistake, not in the sense of a moral failure, but in the nonjudgmental sense of taking one thing for another, taking something for its opposite. Hamartia may betoken an error of discernment due to ignorance, to the lack of an essential piece of information. Finally, hamartia may be viewed simply as an act which, for whatever reason, ends in failure rather than success.[4]

Herein lie the 2019 Phillies in the only way I can understand them, which is not especially illuminating. Injury is the purview of chance, especially as it pertains to players like McCutchen and Robertson, two players who have heretofore enjoyed the lion's share of luck and durability in relation to their bodies and their work. There is no model against the cruel and curious whims of the universe. But if it's hard to pinpoint a sole cause—or even a small group of them—what can be corrected? If, beyond chance, the vast majority of the players on the team perform below expectations—even and especially the ones for whom a team has the highest hopes—in concert, what is to be done?

Well, one thing that was done was to relieve some people of their duties. If it's difficult to make something tangibly better, at least make it different. Hitting coach John Mallee was replaced by Charlie Manuel (in interim capacity) in August and pitching coach Chris Young was let go at season's end. Though much beloved in Philadelphia, Charlie had no swift resolution for the quiet bats (Harper's near-immediate moonshot notwithstanding). No reverse Friar Lawrence here, bearing a potion for waking. And, as seemed inevitable as the regular season ended,

Gabe Kapler, whose managerial stint in Philadelphia died amid the accumulated wreckage of two dismal Septembers, has been replaced. The Phillies chose Joe Girardi.

"Romeo and Juliet" ends with a nod toward peace between the Montagues and Capulets, a peace born of the ugliest kind of failure, but the failure in the play is easy enough to name: vengefulness, pride, and those occasional caprices of the author's hand that move in the guise of chance. Here is the thesis of a thousand sophomore-year essays: success—which is to say peace, harmony, happiness—might have been one interaction away for Juliet and her Romeo. What peace in Philadelphia?

When last Joe Girardi stood meaningfully in a dugout in Citizens Bank Park, it was as the manager of the New York Yankees, en route to a 4-2 triumph in the 2009 World Series. When the Phillies announced Girardi's hiring in October, former Phillies outfielder Shane Victorino welcomed him, saying he was still mad about '09, but he'd forgive him if Girardi could get the current Phillies another championship.[5] It's a joke, and it isn't. The Phillies 2009 World Series loss stands as the edge of a steep downward slope. Not even the frighteningly impressive rotation including Roy Halladay, Cliff Lee, Cole Hamels, and Roy Oswalt could spur the team back to championship play, and there've been no trips to the playoffs at all since 2011.

One may erase a handful of those fruitless years with the word *rebuild*. Those years had a different destination than the one the team declared by signing Harper and McCutchen and acquiring Realmuto an offseason ago. (One may argue that declaring one particular destination—playoff-bound—with an expected rotation of Nola, Arrieta, and a lot of *hope* regarding a handful of pitchers who have never quite managed to execute success for any particular duration, is another oft-cited source of hamartia: hubris. But, as Jules Brody writes, let's call it "failure for whatever reason.")

Regardless of signings and the absence of such, it's the players on the field, the actors on the wide, green stage under so many lights, who have to see the story through. It's going to take a lot of good contact. It's going to take Fortune's favors. It's going to take success, which is to say the cumulative effect of 162 games, which, for whatever reason, end in success, rather than failure. That, and only that, will bury this decade of strife.

—Holly Wendt is an author of Baseball Prospectus.

1. William Shakespeare, "Romeo and Juliet," in The Riverside Shakespeare, 2nd ed. (New York: Houghton Mifflin, 1997), 1104-1139.

  2. Ibid.

  3. Ibid.

  4. Jules Brody, "Fate, Philology, Freud," Philosophy and Literature 38 (2014): 1-29.

5. Philadelphia Phillies, "Photo of Joe Girardi." Instagram, 28 October 2019. Accessed 3 November 2019. https://www.instagram.com/p/B4LYuFzJBmA/?igshid=93486k06b4vj

Part 2: Player Analysis

Philadelphia Phillies 2020

PLAYER COMMENTS WITH GRAPHS

Jay Bruce RF
Born: 04/03/87   Age: 33   Bats: L   Throws: L
Height: 6'3"   Weight: 225   Origin: Round 1, 2005 Draft (#12 overall)

YEAR	TEAM	LVL	AGE	PA	R	2B	3B	HR	RBI	BB	K	SB	CS	AVG/OBP/SLG
2017	NYN	MLB	30	448	61	20	0	29	75	39	102	0	1	.256/.321/.520
2017	CLE	MLB	30	169	21	9	2	7	26	18	37	1	0	.248/.331/.477
2018	SLU	A+	31	27	3	1	0	1	2	2	6	0	0	.360/.407/.520
2018	NYN	MLB	31	361	31	18	1	9	37	41	75	2	3	.223/.310/.370
2019	SEA	MLB	32	184	27	11	0	14	28	16	53	1	0	.212/.283/.533
2019	PHI	MLB	32	149	16	6	0	12	31	3	29	0	0	.221/.235/.510
2020	PHI	MLB	33	238	29	10	1	14	36	19	62	2	1	.212/.278/.453

Comparables: Jesse Barfield, Justin Upton, Wil Myers

Bruce's last two seasons have been so injury riddled that BP's lawyers had to carefully review this comment to make sure it wasn't committing a HIPAA violation. Initially, a change of scenery and leagues seemed to light a fire under Bruce, as he hit seven home runs in his first 12 games for the Mariners, but only two hits of the non-dong variety led to a bizarre .204/.298/.673 line. Before his BABIP could get right, his left Achilles went wrong on April 12, setting off a series of maladies that marred Bruce's season. Traded to the Phillies in early June, he missed time with hamstring, elbow and Achilles (again) injuries before finally landing on the IL on July 17 with a right oblique strain. Upon returning, he lasted exactly one day before a new injury - a left flexor strain for those playing Bruce malady bingo at home - put him back on the shelf and rendered him a 1990's-style pinch hitter the rest of the way. Only 32 on Opening Day, Bruce has what Bill James once described as "old player skills" and while Bruce can still put a charge into the ball, that alone won't allow him to hang around well into his 30s.

YEAR	TEAM	LVL	AGE	PA	DRC+	VORP	BABIP	BRR	FRAA	WARP
2017	NYN	MLB	30	448	115	25.6	.271	0.1	RF(92): 2.3, 1B(11): -0.1	2.0
2017	CLE	MLB	30	169	114	6.9	.283	0.4	RF(41): -2.7, 1B(1): 0.0	0.4
2018	SLU	A+	31	27	139	2.3	.444	0.0	RF(3): -0.4, 1B(3): 0.2	0.1
2018	NYN	MLB	31	361	91	2.2	.263	-1.8	RF(64): -0.6, 1B(21): -0.2	0.0
2019	SEA	MLB	32	184	115	7.2	.210	0.6	RF(24): -1.5, 1B(16): 0.5	1.0
2019	PHI	MLB	32	149	97	3.7	.190	0.1	LF(31): 3.6	0.7
2020	PHI	MLB	33	238	85	1.5	.228	0.0	LF 1, 1B 0	0.3

Jay Bruce, continued

Batted Ball Distribution

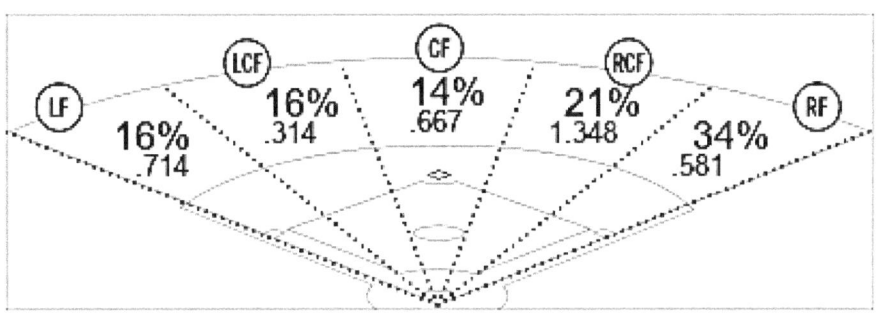

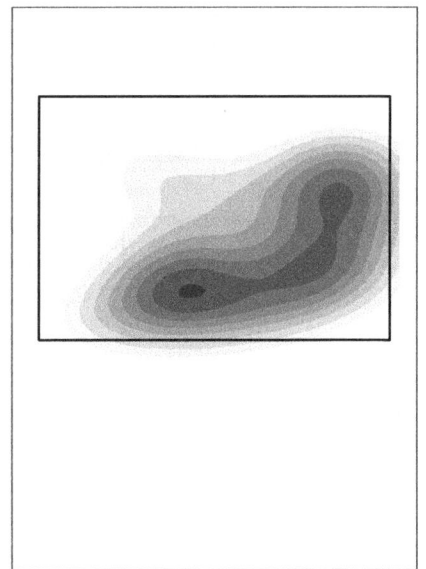

Strike Zone vs LHP

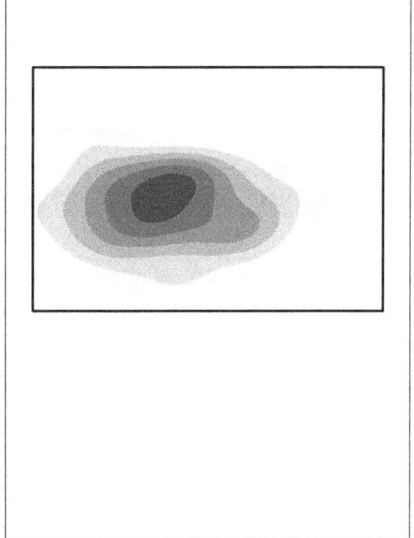

Strike Zone vs RHP

Kyle Garlick OF

Born: 01/26/92   Age: 28   Bats: R   Throws: R
Height: 6'1"   Weight: 210   Origin: Round 28, 2015 Draft (#852 overall)

YEAR	TEAM	LVL	AGE	PA	R	2B	3B	HR	RBI	BB	K	SB	CS	AVG/OBP/SLG
2017	TUL	AA	25	305	45	9	0	17	42	30	78	1	0	.239/.321/.463
2018	TUL	AA	26	85	11	4	0	5	14	6	33	0	0	.282/.329/.526
2018	OKL	AAA	26	341	49	18	2	17	46	14	105	2	0	.253/.287/.478
2019	OKL	AAA	27	304	54	25	2	23	59	25	84	2	1	.314/.382/.675
2019	LAN	MLB	27	53	8	4	0	3	6	5	19	0	0	.250/.321/.521
2020	LAN	MLB	28	42	4	2	0	2	5	3	14	0	0	.218/.276/.400

Comparables: Andrew Brown, Brad Glenn, Keon Broxton

It's a testament to both Garlick himself and the Dodgers player development machine that he gets more than a lineout in this book. Most 27-year-old organizational depth pieces get a cursory nod and nothing more. Of course, Garlick proved to be something more than that, slugging nearly 100 points better than league average in limited time. Most organizational depth pieces don't lead the majors in any category, but Garlick again proved something more by averaging 245 feet in batted ball distance (Joey Gallo eat your heart out). The Dodgers didn't really need another random player to turn into a viable major leaguer, but it just goes to show that a little bit of Garlick can enhance just about anything.

YEAR	TEAM	LVL	AGE	PA	DRC+	VORP	BABIP	BRR	FRAA	WARP
2017	TUL	AA	25	305	113	8.0	.267	0.9	LF(43): -1.2, RF(23): 3.8	1.4
2018	TUL	AA	26	85	77	3.3	.415	0.6	RF(8): -0.2, LF(8): 1.7	0.2
2018	OKL	AAA	26	341	83	9.2	.320	-1.2	RF(58): 3.9, LF(26): -1.4	0.2
2019	OKL	AAA	27	304	139	29.1	.373	-0.8	RF(47): -0.2, LF(23): -3.6	1.6
2019	LAN	MLB	27	53	87	0.6	.346	0.2	LF(12): 0.3, RF(5): -0.2	0.1
2020	LAN	MLB	28	42	75	-0.2	.293	-0.1	LF 0	0.0

Kyle Garlick, continued

Batted Ball Distribution

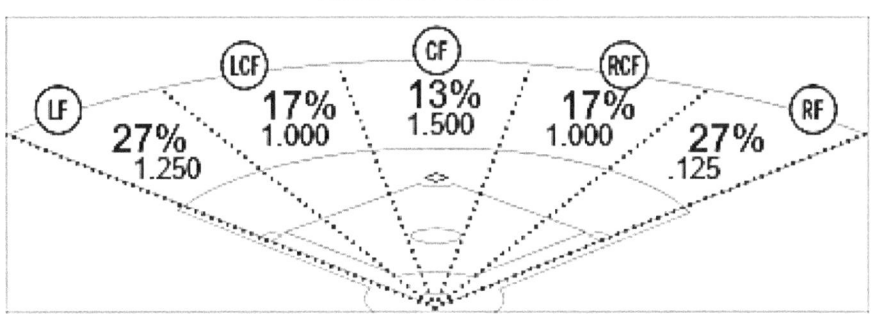

Strike Zone vs LHP   **Strike Zone vs RHP**

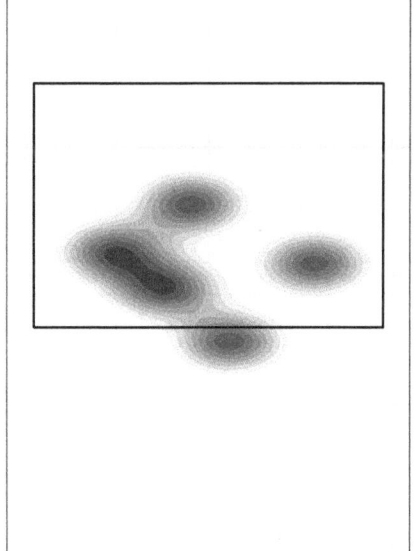

Phillies Player Analysis - 27

Didi Gregorius SS

Born: 02/18/90 Age: 30 Bats: L Throws: R
Height: 6'3" Weight: 205 Origin: International Free Agent, 2007

YEAR	TEAM	LVL	AGE	PA	R	2B	3B	HR	RBI	BB	K	SB	CS	AVG/OBP/SLG
2017	NYA	MLB	27	570	73	27	0	25	87	25	70	3	1	.287/.318/.478
2018	NYA	MLB	28	569	89	23	5	27	86	48	69	10	6	.268/.335/.494
2019	NYA	MLB	29	344	47	14	2	16	61	17	53	2	1	.238/.276/.441
2020	PHI	MLB	30	560	61	25	2	21	71	32	92	6	2	.243/.294/.421

Comparables: Marwin Gonzalez, Freddy Galvis, Eduardo Escobar

Sir Didi, The Knight in shining pinstripes, spent his last year donning the iconic uniform and he went out, not with a bang, but a whimper. Fighting back from Tommy John surgery, it was an open question as to whether or not Gregorius would be the same player he was before: a smooth-fielding shortstop with newly acquired lefty power. And while the power still flashed, it was an unfortunate façade as his approach returned to its pre-2018 days and his defense unraveled. The truncated recovery time and lack of spring training certainly played a role in his lackluster performance, but with Gleyber Torres locked into the six, there was no need for the Yankees to find out exactly how much positive regression can be expected first-hand.

YEAR	TEAM	LVL	AGE	PA	DRC+	VORP	BABIP	BRR	FRAA	WARP
2017	NYA	MLB	27	570	115	38.4	.287	1.9	SS(135): 4.9	4.4
2018	NYA	MLB	28	569	121	40.3	.259	2.3	SS(132): 0.4	4.4
2019	NYA	MLB	29	344	96	14.9	.237	1.0	SS(80): -7.3	0.8
2020	PHI	MLB	30	560	87	13.0	.258	1.8	SS 1, 2B 0	1.4

Didi Gregorius, continued

Batted Ball Distribution

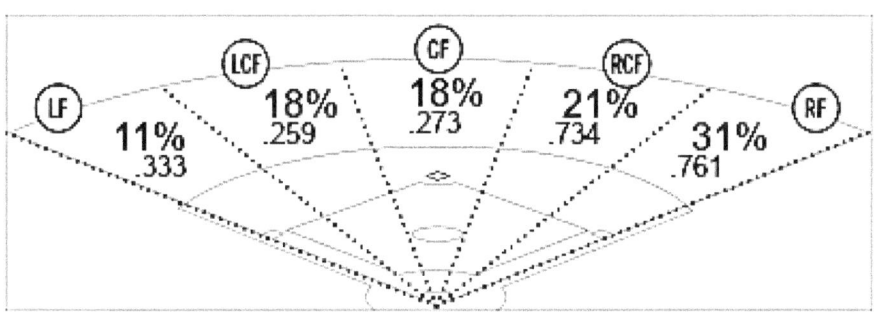

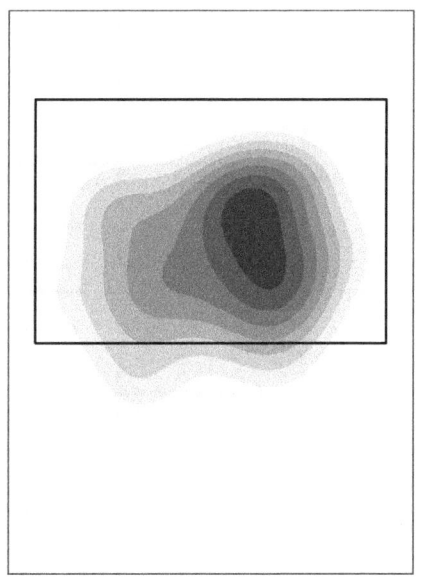

Strike Zone vs LHP

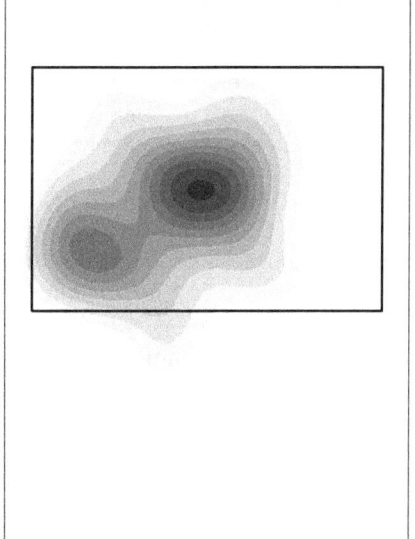

Strike Zone vs RHP

Philadelphia Phillies 2020

Bryce Harper RF

Born: 10/16/92   Age: 27   Bats: L   Throws: R
Height: 6'3"   Weight: 220   Origin: Round 1, 2010 Draft (#1 overall)

YEAR	TEAM	LVL	AGE	PA	R	2B	3B	HR	RBI	BB	K	SB	CS	AVG/OBP/SLG
2017	WAS	MLB	24	492	95	27	1	29	87	68	99	4	2	.319/.413/.595
2018	WAS	MLB	25	695	103	34	0	34	100	130	169	13	3	.249/.393/.496
2019	PHI	MLB	26	682	98	36	1	35	114	99	178	15	3	.260/.372/.510
2020	PHI	MLB	27	595	86	27	1	32	91	92	149	9	4	.254/.374/.502

Comparables: Boog Powell, Matt Joyce, Willie Horton

Year One of the Bryce Harper Era in The City of Brotherly Love felt like an anticlimax, an inaugural season that was somehow very good yet simultaneously unremarkable. Even the press conference in early March anointing of the next great face of the franchise played like the end of a reality television show that had been on the air far too long and provided its disinterested audience a clumsy, ham-handed and disappointing ending. Baseball isn't dying (even though the constant chirping of the nattering nabobs might make some believe otherwise), but it also isn't the preeminent and dominant sport it was a generation ago. It isn't his fault, but Harper is a superstar who belongs in a different age, an era that would have had a greater appreciation for his personality and a fanbase unaware of WARP and DRC+ that could instead marvel at what he is instead of nitpicking what he isn't.

Even this milquetoast "what Bryce Harper is" qualifier is more than a little disingenuous. He isn't a slice of stinky cheese sitting atop a slice of moldy, day old bread; since his debut in 2012 Harper is sixth in runs scored, eighth in on-base percentage and ninth in home runs across the majors. He's even one of the clutchest hitters there is, with a WPA that's sixth-best in baseball over that span. But even if you are adamant about using a nerd stat like WARP as Harper's definitive yardstick, he's still pretty damn good, the 29th best age 26 and under hitter since integration, ranked mostly behind a bushel of Hall of Famers, active or recently retired players who will be Hall of Famers and PED or alleged PED users who will never be enshrined. Harper is sometimes painted with a harsh brush that says he's a lousy teammate, a malcontent or a player who doesn't try hard enough. But he is none of those things. What he is is a player who is incessantly penalized for not being Mantle, A-Rod, Griffey, Aaron or even his own generation's version of those guys: Mike Trout.

There is a parallel universe where baseball still reigns supreme, kids gush over boxscores, and Harper is part of a lively discussion among ardent fans over where he belongs in the game's pantheon. It's the jaded world that surrounds Harper - and not his accomplishments on the field - that have reduced him into someone who recedes into the background and is blamed for what he isn't instead of celebrated for everything that he is.

YEAR	TEAM	LVL	AGE	PA	DRC+	VORP	BABIP	BRR	FRAA	WARP
2017	WAS	MLB	24	492	147	47.2	.356	-1.3	RF(110): -3.4	3.5
2018	WAS	MLB	25	695	126	53.0	.289	-3.2	RF(116): -12.1, CF(63): -0.1	2.5
2019	PHI	MLB	26	682	122	36.0	.313	-1.4	RF(152): 3.7	3.7
2020	*PHI*	*MLB*	*27*	*595*	*127*	*31.9*	*.298*	*-2.3*	*RF -7*	*2.6*

Bryce Harper, continued

Batted Ball Distribution

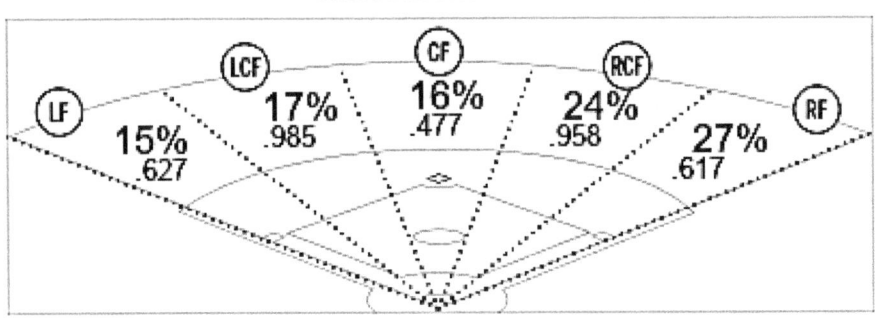

Strike Zone vs LHP   Strike Zone vs RHP

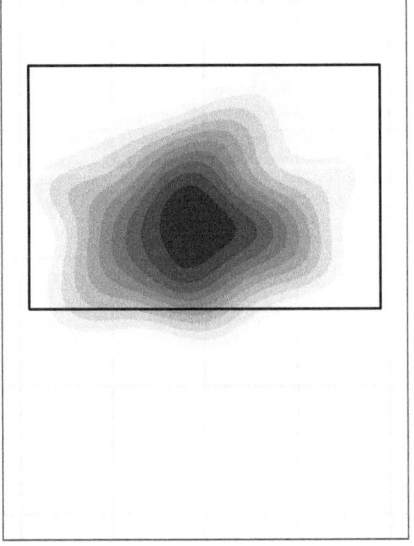

Josh Harrison 2B

Born: 07/08/87 Age: 32 Bats: R Throws: R
Height: 5'8" Weight: 185 Origin: Round 6, 2008 Draft (#191 overall)

YEAR	TEAM	LVL	AGE	PA	R	2B	3B	HR	RBI	BB	K	SB	CS	AVG/OBP/SLG
2017	PIT	MLB	29	542	66	26	2	16	47	28	90	12	4	.272/.339/.432
2018	PIT	MLB	30	374	41	13	1	8	37	18	68	3	0	.250/.293/.363
2019	TOL	AAA	31	29	2	1	0	0	3	6	4	0	0	.174/.345/.217
2019	DET	MLB	31	147	10	7	1	1	8	6	27	4	2	.175/.218/.263
2020	PHI	MLB	32	294	27	13	1	6	29	15	56	6	2	.234/.285/.360

Comparables: Luis Salazar, Terry Pendleton, Brock Holt

Everybody knows Achilles had one weakness and it was a spot on his heel. What mythologians rarely discuss is the Greek hero of Hamstring, one of the fastest and most energetic warriors who suddenly missed significant time on the battlefield because he pulled up lame one day. Thousands of years later, Harrison suffered a similar injury during a bizarre 2019 season that saw him signed during spring training and released at the end of his rehab assignment because his position had been filled. Never one for walking and seldom one for bopping, his on-field contributions are tied to his energy, defensive flexibility and mobility—and, if he hits a snag and loses any of those attributes, then he's just another tragedy. Have you read the essay at the beginning of this chapter? He'll fit in perfectly with the Phillies.

YEAR	TEAM	LVL	AGE	PA	DRC+	VORP	BABIP	BRR	FRAA	WARP
2017	PIT	MLB	29	542	105	31.8	.303	1.7	2B(83): -2.6, 3B(49): 2.6	2.2
2018	PIT	MLB	30	374	87	3.2	.286	0.5	2B(87): -5.6, 3B(2): 0.0	0.0
2019	TOL	AAA	31	29	105	-1.5	.211	-0.9	2B(3): -0.1	0.0
2019	DET	MLB	31	147	63	-2.2	.207	-1.1	2B(34): 2.7	-0.1
2020	PHI	MLB	32	294	70	-1.4	.272	0.1	2B -1, 3B 0	-0.2

Josh Harrison, continued

Batted Ball Distribution

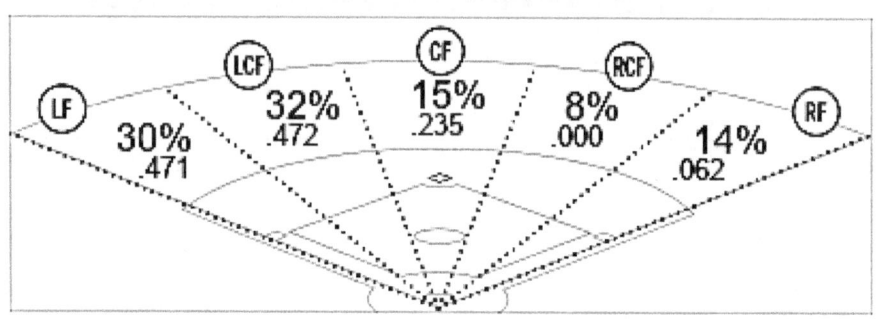

LF	LCF	CF	RCF	RF
30% .471	32% .472	15% .235	8% .000	14% .062

Strike Zone vs LHP

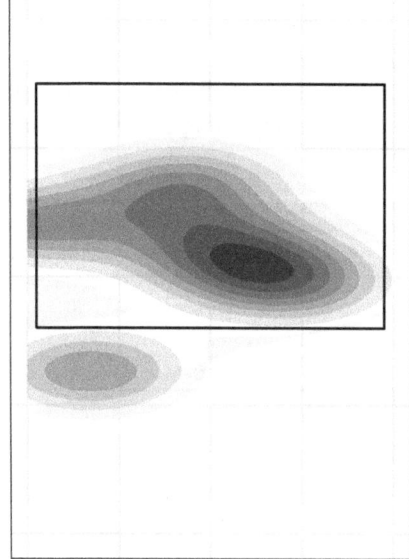

Strike Zone vs RHP

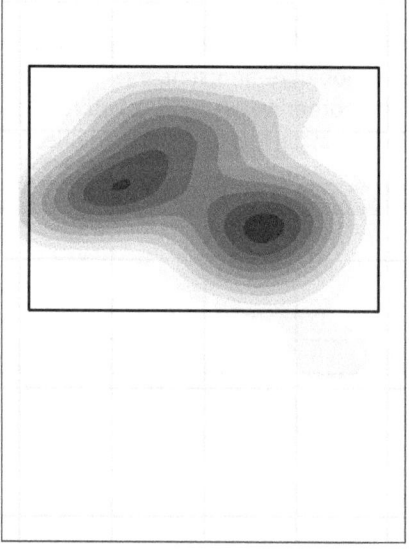

Adam Haseley CF

Born: 04/12/96   Age: 24   Bats: L   Throws: L
Height: 6'1"   Weight: 195   Origin: Round 1, 2017 Draft (#8 overall)

YEAR	TEAM	LVL	AGE	PA	R	2B	3B	HR	RBI	BB	K	SB	CS	AVG/OBP/SLG
2017	WPT	A-	21	158	18	9	0	2	18	14	28	5	3	.270/.350/.380
2017	LWD	A	21	74	15	3	1	1	6	6	13	0	1	.258/.315/.379
2018	CLR	A+	22	354	54	13	5	5	38	19	54	7	3	.300/.343/.415
2018	REA	AA	22	159	23	4	0	6	17	16	19	0	1	.316/.403/.478
2019	REA	AA	23	190	30	8	2	8	21	21	35	4	2	.267/.353/.485
2019	LEH	AAA	23	78	8	6	0	2	9	8	14	1	1	.294/.377/.471
2019	PHI	MLB	23	242	30	14	0	5	26	14	60	4	0	.266/.324/.396
2020	PHI	MLB	24	364	36	16	1	10	39	26	87	2	1	.241/.305/.380

Comparables: Cedric Mullins, Preston Tucker, Carlos González

Haseley is a solid defender and a good contact hitter with a discerning eye but one can't help thinking he'd be better served by a DeLorean and an eccentric scientist from Hill Valley. Haseley's heavy ground-ball profile isn't a great fit in a version of the game where balls are escaping the yard at a prodigious rate. To his credit, he has worked arduously with the Phillies' coaching staff at multiple levels of the organization to adjust his swing, but this is a tough trick to turn on the fly, particularly when the plan was for Haseley to spend all of 2019 at Lehigh Valley before injuries forced the team's hand. The former first-rounder was an adequate hitter out of the gate before he became too pull happy, resulting in even more grounders. He's young enough to believe tangible improvement is possible, but one can't help thinking Haseley is an anachronism in a game where 20-25 home run power is a prerequisite for a starting outfielder without game breaking speed.

YEAR	TEAM	LVL	AGE	PA	DRC+	VORP	BABIP	BRR	FRAA	WARP
2017	WPT	A-	21	158	134	12.9	.321	2.6	CF(31): 0.1	1.2
2017	LWD	A	21	74	108	5.9	.302	1.6	LF(12): 1.3, CF(4): 0.8	0.6
2018	CLR	A+	22	354	109	15.2	.346	2.9	LF(39): -2.5, CF(30): -2.2	1.4
2018	REA	AA	22	159	135	13.1	.327	-0.5	CF(28): -2.3, RF(5): -0.5	0.7
2019	REA	AA	23	190	120	15.2	.290	2.1	RF(23): 1.3, CF(19): -1.8	1.0
2019	LEH	AAA	23	78	116	4.1	.346	-0.8	CF(12): -0.4, LF(5): 0.1	0.3
2019	PHI	MLB	23	242	71	-1.4	.344	1.1	CF(40): -3.9, LF(22): 2.0	-0.2
2020	PHI	MLB	24	364	82	4.0	.299	0.3	CF -4, RF 1	0.1

Philadelphia Phillies 2020

Adam Haseley, continued

Batted Ball Distribution

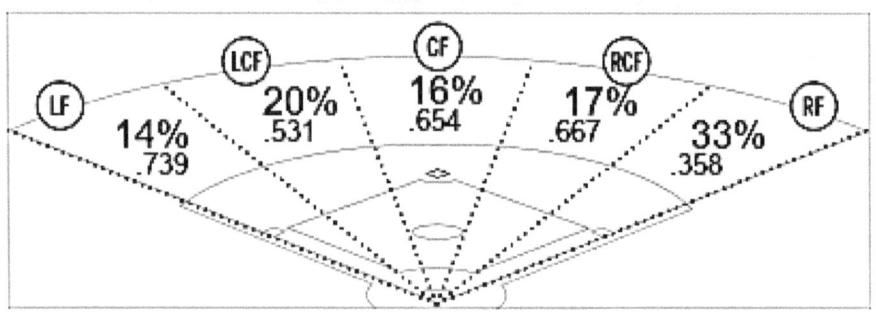

Strike Zone vs LHP   **Strike Zone vs RHP**

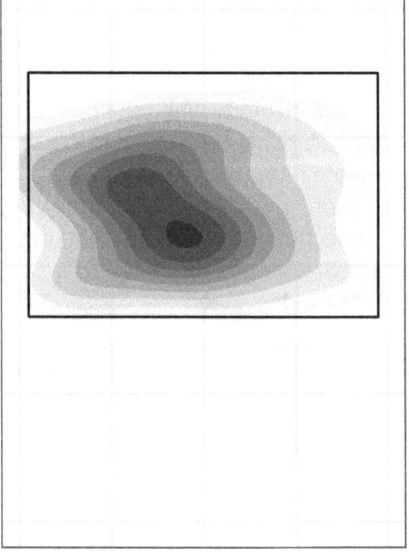

Odúbel Herrera CF

Born: 12/29/91   Age: 28   Bats: L   Throws: R
Height: 5'11"   Weight: 205   Origin: International Free Agent, 2008

YEAR	TEAM	LVL	AGE	PA	R	2B	3B	HR	RBI	BB	K	SB	CS	AVG/OBP/SLG
2017	PHI	MLB	25	563	67	42	3	14	56	31	126	8	5	.281/.325/.452
2018	PHI	MLB	26	597	64	19	3	22	71	38	122	5	2	.255/.310/.420
2019	PHI	MLB	27	139	12	10	1	1	16	11	33	2	2	.222/.288/.341
2020	PHI	MLB	28	119	12	5	1	3	14	9	29	2	1	.248/.308/.401

Comparables: Milton Bradley, Carlos Beltrán, Carlos Gómez

On May 27, 2019, Herrera was arrested and charged with assault in Atlantic City after allegedly attacking his then 20-year-old girlfriend. A criminal assault case was dropped by the District Attorney's office in early July because the victim decided not to press charges. After conducting their own investigation of the incident, Major League Baseball suspended Herrera for 85 games, retroactive to June 24, ending his season. This spring, scribes might wax poetic about Herrera's return to the baseball diamond. A few may even misguidedly opine about his difficult road, idiotically conflating his return from a justified, deserved suspension with overcoming personal adversity. Herrera could have a great or awful year on the diamond. It will be meaningless compared to the damage he did to the health and well-being of his victim, something that is all too easily and quickly forgotten. This happens far too frequently where domestic violence is concerned.

YEAR	TEAM	LVL	AGE	PA	DRC+	VORP	BABIP	BRR	FRAA	WARP
2017	PHI	MLB	25	563	90	21.3	.345	-1.8	CF(133): 10.5	2.1
2018	PHI	MLB	26	597	93	21.3	.290	0.8	CF(133): -1.1, RF(9): -1.2	1.4
2019	PHI	MLB	27	139	70	-0.3	.290	-1.2	CF(37): -2.1	-0.3
2020	PHI	MLB	28	119	86	2.2	.307	-0.1	CF 1	0.3

Odúbel Herrera, continued

Batted Ball Distribution

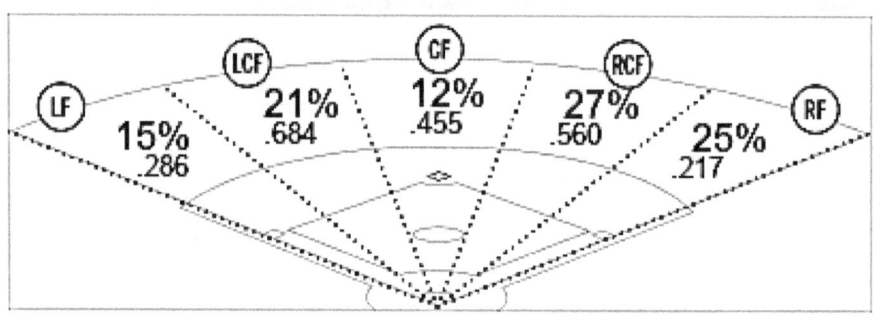

Strike Zone vs LHP Strike Zone vs RHP

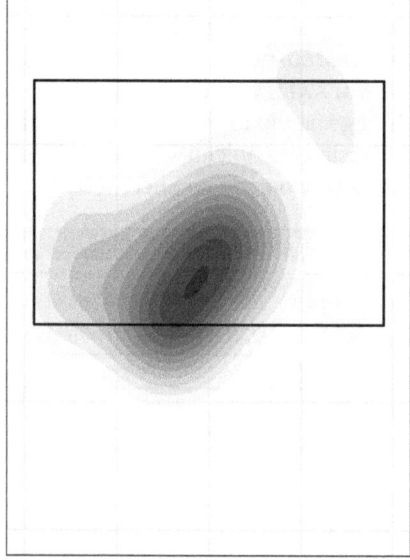

Rhys Hoskins 1B

Born: 03/17/93   Age: 27   Bats: R   Throws: R
Height: 6'4"   Weight: 225   Origin: Round 5, 2014 Draft (#142 overall)

YEAR	TEAM	LVL	AGE	PA	R	2B	3B	HR	RBI	BB	K	SB	CS	AVG/OBP/SLG
2017	LEH	AAA	24	475	78	24	4	29	91	64	75	4	2	.284/.385/.581
2017	PHI	MLB	24	212	37	7	0	18	48	37	46	2	0	.259/.396/.618
2018	PHI	MLB	25	660	89	38	0	34	96	87	150	5	3	.246/.354/.496
2019	PHI	MLB	26	705	86	33	5	29	85	116	173	2	2	.226/.364/.454
2020	PHI	MLB	27	595	82	26	2	31	89	88	143	3	1	.237/.360/.483

Comparables: Michael Conforto, Brandon Allen, Mike Olt

Like Walt Whitman in his Leaves of Grass anthology, Hoskins contained multitudes. After posting a blistering .931 OPS before the All-Star break (good for 14th overall among qualifiers), Hoskins cratered, posting a woeful .180/.318/.361 line in the second half. Hoskins' contact rate didn't change much, but his quality of contact was far poorer after the break. He had trouble getting around on fastballs and the pull approach that was such a significant part of Hoskins' game gave way to a more straightaway swing that didn't serve him well. A hand injury in August might have had an impact, but the slump started in mid-July well before the malady occurred. Hoskins didn't drop off the way some of his teammates did in 2019, but the Phillies lack right-handed power and need him to show up in 2020 with all his laser beams full-dazzling.

YEAR	TEAM	LVL	AGE	PA	DRC+	VORP	BABIP	BRR	FRAA	WARP
2017	LEH	AAA	24	475	162	36.4	.281	-0.6	1B(105): -9.8, LF(3): 0.2	2.5
2017	PHI	MLB	24	212	151	26.5	.241	-0.1	LF(30): -0.8, 1B(27): -0.3	1.6
2018	PHI	MLB	25	660	129	48.1	.272	0.2	LF(135): -0.7, 1B(17): 0.2	3.9
2019	PHI	MLB	26	705	115	24.3	.267	-2.3	1B(158): 2.6	2.4
2020	PHI	MLB	27	595	120	26.4	.268	-0.6	1B 0	2.8

Philadelphia Phillies 2020

Rhys Hoskins, continued

Batted Ball Distribution

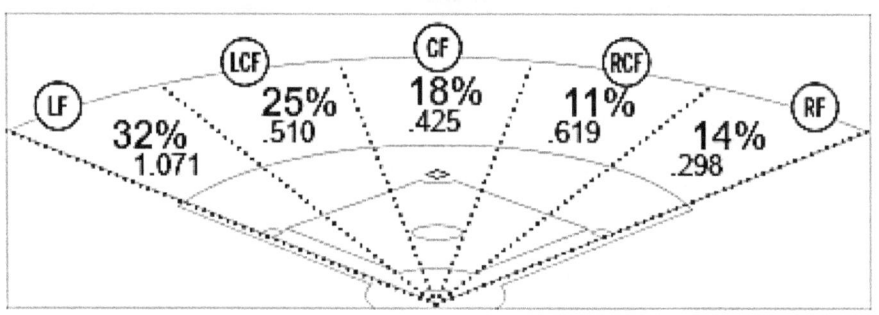

Strike Zone vs LHP   **Strike Zone vs RHP**

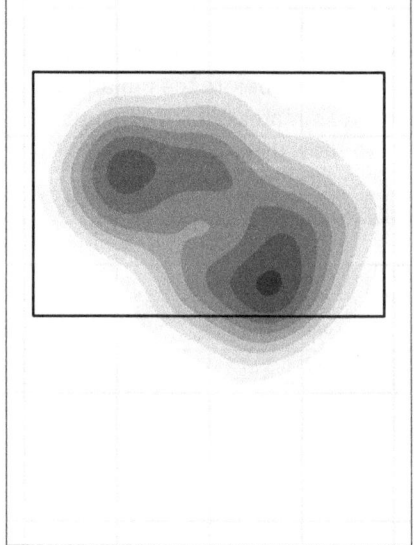

Scott Kingery CF

Born: 04/29/94 Age: 26 Bats: R Throws: R
Height: 5'10" Weight: 180 Origin: Round 2, 2015 Draft (#48 overall)

YEAR	TEAM	LVL	AGE	PA	R	2B	3B	HR	RBI	BB	K	SB	CS	AVG/OBP/SLG
2017	REA	AA	23	317	62	18	5	18	44	28	51	19	3	.313/.379/.608
2017	LEH	AAA	23	286	41	11	3	8	21	13	58	10	2	.294/.337/.449
2018	PHI	MLB	24	484	55	23	2	8	35	24	126	10	3	.226/.267/.338
2019	PHI	MLB	25	500	64	34	4	19	55	34	147	15	4	.258/.315/.474
2020	PHI	MLB	26	532	54	23	3	18	62	31	151	12	3	.228/.282/.392

Comparables: Eddie Miksis, Tom Upton, Don Zimmer

There was nowhere to go but up after a miserable rookie campaign, so by this admittedly low bar, Kingery's sophomore season was a rousing success. The former Arizona Wildcat took a more aggressive approach in his second go-round, swinging earlier in the count and attacking pitchers instead of falling behind and taking defensive swings. On the other side of the ball, Kingery adapted well to a super utility role, playing multiple positions capably and giving the Phillies an opportunity to give several veterans a breather throughout the season. The downside of Kingery's year is while he did show marked improvement, he was merely a two-win player who was slightly below average offensively. Kingery is likely to be a fixture for years to come, but the excitement fueled by a strong season in an extremely hitter-friendly minor league environment appears to have been overblown.

YEAR	TEAM	LVL	AGE	PA	DRC+	VORP	BABIP	BRR	FRAA	WARP
2017	REA	AA	23	317	147	33.9	.324	2.7	2B(59): 1.7	3.0
2017	LEH	AAA	23	286	111	9.7	.348	-1.2	2B(54): 0.9, 3B(4): 0.3	1.2
2018	PHI	MLB	24	484	70	4.5	.291	2.1	SS(119): -3.9, 3B(10): -0.2	0.2
2019	PHI	MLB	25	500	93	14.9	.337	3.1	CF(65): -2.2, 3B(41): 1.4	1.9
2020	PHI	MLB	26	532	74	0.1	.292	2.1	3B 4, CF -1	0.4

Philadelphia Phillies 2020

Scott Kingery, continued

Batted Ball Distribution

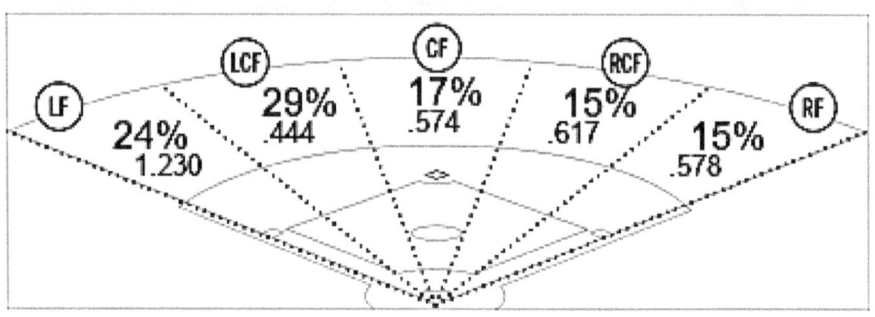

Strike Zone vs LHP   **Strike Zone vs RHP**

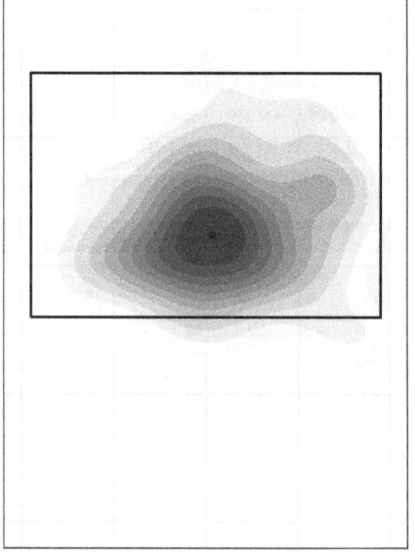

Nick Martini LF

Born: 06/27/90 Age: 30 Bats: L Throws: L
Height: 5'11" Weight: 205 Origin: Round 7, 2011 Draft (#230 overall)

YEAR	TEAM	LVL	AGE	PA	R	2B	3B	HR	RBI	BB	K	SB	CS	AVG/OBP/SLG
2017	SFD	AA	27	110	13	5	0	2	15	11	16	1	0	.263/.336/.374
2017	MEM	AAA	27	426	60	20	5	6	55	55	77	5	1	.303/.394/.436
2018	NAS	AAA	28	330	44	12	2	6	40	51	68	5	1	.297/.406/.420
2018	OAK	MLB	28	179	26	9	3	1	19	21	36	0	0	.296/.397/.414
2019	LVG	AAA	29	329	57	18	0	8	42	49	51	0	0	.328/.432/.482
2019	SDN	MLB	29	96	7	4	1	0	5	12	21	0	0	.244/.344/.317
2019	OAK	MLB	29	13	1	0	0	1	2	2	5	0	0	.091/.231/.364
2020	CIN	MLB	30	7	1	0	0	0	1	1	2	0	0	.247/.342/.367

Comparables: David Freitas, Robbie Grossman, Darin Mastroianni

If you read *Moneyball*, you might well have thought Martini and his on-base-centric approach was the Platonic ideal of a *Moneyball* player. And when Billy Beane's Athletics released him last August, you would have been shocked, since you clearly misunderstood both *Moneyball* and the concept of a Platonic ideal. Martini caught on with the Padres and provided them with his usual mix of punchless patience and competent defense in an outfield corner, making him perfectly suited for a big-league bench role. He's the heir apparent to another factory second from the St. Louis assembly line, Jon Jay, whose similar lefty on-base skills and reputation for professional at-bats has kept him hitting white balls for batting practice well into his mid-30s.

YEAR	TEAM	LVL	AGE	PA	DRC+	VORP	BABIP	BRR	FRAA	WARP
2017	SFD	AA	27	110	113	5.4	.296	0.9	LF(16): 1.9, RF(3): 0.7	0.7
2017	MEM	AAA	27	426	121	29.6	.363	1.2	LF(53): -0.3, RF(24): 0.6	2.3
2018	NAS	AAA	28	330	128	23.3	.373	2.5	1B(41): 2.8, LF(22): 0.2	2.4
2018	OAK	MLB	28	179	104	14.0	.379	1.1	LF(47): 2.1, CF(2): 0.2	0.9
2019	LVG	AAA	29	329	122	18.8	.376	-1.3	LF(51): -8.8	0.8
2019	SDN	MLB	29	96	80	0.1	.323	-0.4	LF(23): 0.6	0.0
2019	OAK	MLB	29	13	79	0.1	.000	0.0	LF(3): 0.1, P(1): 0.0	0.0
2020	CIN	MLB	30	7	92	0.2	.310	0.0	LF 0, 1B 0	0.0

Nick Martini, continued

Batted Ball Distribution

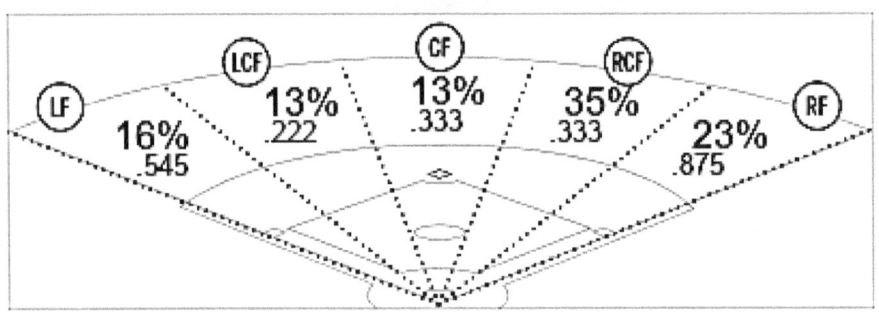

Strike Zone vs LHP   **Strike Zone vs RHP**

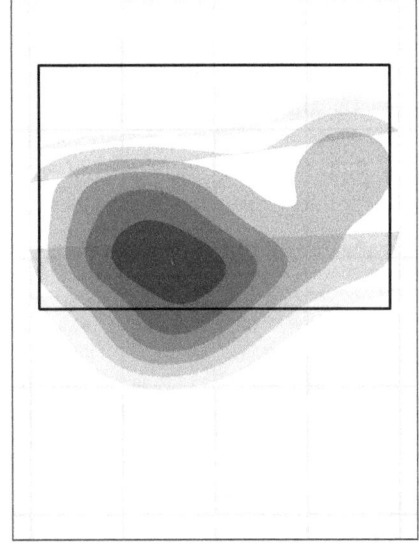

Andrew McCutchen   LF

Born: 10/10/86   Age: 33   Bats: R   Throws: R
Height: 5'11"   Weight: 195   Origin: Round 1, 2005 Draft (#11 overall)

YEAR	TEAM	LVL	AGE	PA	R	2B	3B	HR	RBI	BB	K	SB	CS	AVG/OBP/SLG
2017	PIT	MLB	30	650	94	30	2	28	88	73	116	11	5	.279/.363/.486
2018	SFN	MLB	31	568	65	28	2	15	55	73	123	13	6	.255/.357/.415
2018	NYA	MLB	31	114	18	2	1	5	10	22	22	1	3	.253/.421/.471
2019	PHI	MLB	32	262	45	12	1	10	29	43	55	2	1	.256/.378/.457
2020	PHI	MLB	33	490	62	19	2	19	63	69	110	8	4	.250/.364/.438

Comparables: Chris Young, Colby Rasmus, Ken Griffey Jr.

It's impossible to talk about Cutch's 2019 without mentioning the horrific injury that abruptly ended his season on June 3; the torn ACL suffered in a rundown that wouldn't have happened if teammate Jean Segura hadn't slipped in the batter's box. Entering the year, McCutchen was the only player in baseball to play at least 146 games in all nine seasons from 2010 to 2018. Even as his performance had somewhat given ground to Father Time, he had managed to stay on the field and soldier on as a productive mainstay. The Phillies missed McCutchen's on-base ability in the second half, but also missed his quiet leadership on and off the field. Cutch is expected to be back at full strength by Opening Day. While he's a long way removed from his halcyon days of MVP, Silver Slugger and Gold Glove awards, Cutch is set to resume his role as table setter and mentor up where the Delaware hits the Schuylkill in 2020.

YEAR	TEAM	LVL	AGE	PA	DRC+	VORP	BABIP	BRR	FRAA	WARP
2017	PIT	MLB	30	650	124	48.7	.305	1.0	CF(139): -10.4, RF(13): -0.8	3.1
2018	SFN	MLB	31	568	116	22.9	.309	-3.7	RF(128): -4.9	1.4
2018	NYA	MLB	31	114	121	8.9	.279	0.3	RF(15): -1.9, LF(12): 0.0	0.4
2019	PHI	MLB	32	262	108	10.3	.299	0.0	LF(52): -0.8, CF(15): -0.7	0.9
2020	PHI	MLB	33	490	113	21.0	.298	-0.6	LF -3	1.9

Philadelphia Phillies 2020

Andrew McCutchen, continued

Batted Ball Distribution

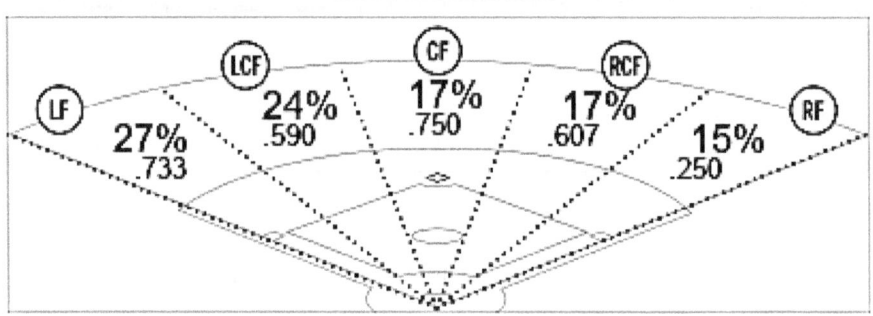

| | **Strike Zone vs LHP** | **Strike Zone vs RHP** |

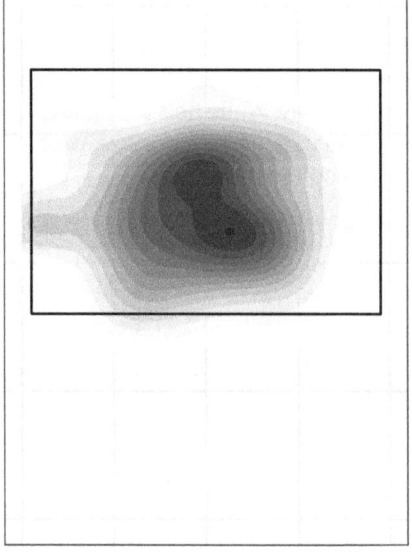

Roman Quinn   OF

Born: 05/14/93   Age: 27   Bats: B   Throws: R
Height: 5'10"   Weight: 170   Origin: Round 2, 2011 Draft (#66 overall)

YEAR	TEAM	LVL	AGE	PA	R	2B	3B	HR	RBI	BB	K	SB	CS	AVG/OBP/SLG
2017	LEH	AAA	24	197	24	8	3	2	13	18	49	10	4	.274/.344/.389
2018	LEH	AAA	25	107	14	2	3	2	11	8	19	13	1	.296/.349/.439
2018	PHI	MLB	25	143	13	6	4	2	12	10	35	10	4	.260/.317/.412
2019	CLR	A+	26	25	6	3	0	1	1	3	6	2	0	.500/.565/.800
2019	PHI	MLB	26	122	18	3	1	4	11	12	34	8	0	.213/.298/.370
2020	PHI	MLB	27	224	22	8	2	5	22	18	63	13	4	.231/.300/.358

Comparables: Dick Kokos, Ben Gamel, Dalton Pompey

Quinn has two problems: he can't stay healthy and on the rare occasions he manages to stay healthy he isn't very good. This is somewhat hyperbolic and unfair. The speedster has shown flashes of the ability that made him a second-round pick by the Phillies in 2011, but he doesn't have enough pop to survive the contemporary version of the game, unless one wants to really buy into his 1.139 August OPS. (Small sample sizes can have severe side effects like vomiting, nausea and overdrafting in fantasy leagues.) Quinn might be helped by baseball's newly expanded rosters in 2020 but it's more likely he'll be a fringe bench player who spends most of his time bouncing between the majors, Triple-A and the injured list yet again.

YEAR	TEAM	LVL	AGE	PA	DRC+	VORP	BABIP	BRR	FRAA	WARP
2017	LEH	AAA	24	197	91	9.9	.368	3.8	CF(38): -0.4, LF(4): -0.2	0.7
2018	LEH	AAA	25	107	104	6.7	.351	3.5	CF(21): 0.3, RF(2): -0.2	0.7
2018	PHI	MLB	25	143	82	4.0	.340	-0.9	CF(30): 0.9, RF(5): 1.3	0.3
2019	CLR	A+	26	25	198	6.2	.692	0.3	CF(5): 0.3	0.4
2019	PHI	MLB	26	122	68	-0.3	.271	0.3	CF(34): -0.6, P(2): 0.0	-0.1
2020	PHI	MLB	27	224	77	1.3	.311	-0.5	CF 2	0.4

Roman Quinn, continued

Batted Ball Distribution

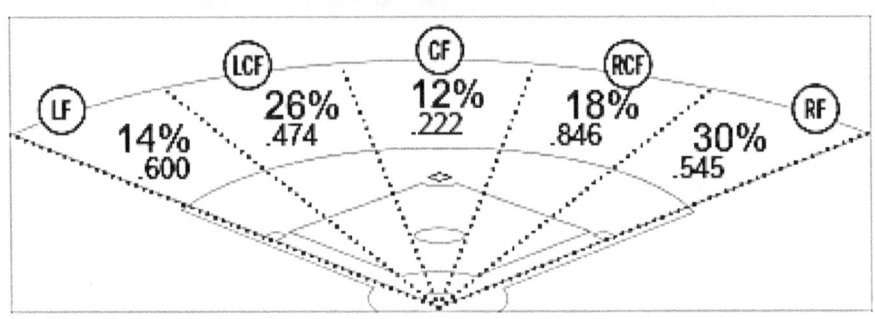

Strike Zone vs LHP **Strike Zone vs RHP**

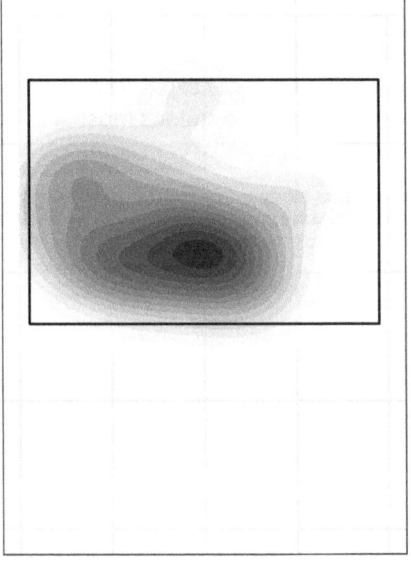

J.T. Realmuto C
Born: 03/18/91   Age: 29   Bats: R   Throws: R
Height: 6'1"   Weight: 210   Origin: Round 3, 2010 Draft (#104 overall)

YEAR	TEAM	LVL	AGE	PA	R	2B	3B	HR	RBI	BB	K	SB	CS	AVG/OBP/SLG
2017	MIA	MLB	26	579	68	31	5	17	65	36	106	8	2	.278/.332/.451
2018	MIA	MLB	27	531	74	30	3	21	74	38	104	3	2	.277/.340/.484
2019	PHI	MLB	28	593	92	36	3	25	83	41	123	9	1	.275/.328/.493
2020	PHI	MLB	29	560	66	29	3	23	76	37	119	7	3	.267/.322/.467

Comparables: Tucker Barnhart, Mike Macfarlane, Miguel Montero

YEAR	TEAM	P. COUNT	FRM RUNS	BLK RUNS	THRW RUNS	TOT RUNS
2017	MIA	18959	5.3	1.7	1.0	9.1
2018	MIA	16399	-0.4	0.9	0.1	0.4
2019	PHI	19166	10.5	4.8	4.7	20.4
2020	PHI	23851	-0.5	1.8	4.8	6.1

The Phillies 2019 season was a story of minor frustrations multiplied to the nth degree, death by a million microscopic cuts, a season that should have and could have been great but instead was decidedly mediocre. Within the framework of several decisions that didn't quite work out or blew up entirely, Realmuto stands out as a gigantic victory. Acquired from the Marlins last February for the considerable cost of Jorge Alfaro and Sixto Sánchez, all he did his first year in the City of Brotherly Love was have a season for the ages, providing elite value behind the dish while also providing strong contributions with the stick. Already a very good player with Miami, Realmuto took it to the next level, putting together a top-10 season among NL hitters and positioning himself for down-ballot MVP votes. The cost of Alfaro and Sanchez might be lamented by Phillies fans half a decade from now but it's difficult if not impossible to kvetch about the short-term impact of a player who delivered in spades by elevating his game to an even higher level.

YEAR	TEAM	LVL	AGE	PA	DRC+	VORP	BABIP	BRR	FRAA	WARP
2017	MIA	MLB	26	579	101	37.5	.318	1.0	C(126): 15.8, 1B(9): 0.3	4.5
2018	MIA	MLB	27	531	122	51.7	.312	4.1	C(112): 3.7, 1B(13): 0.6	4.8
2019	PHI	MLB	28	593	106	35.3	.309	2.1	C(133): 19.5, 1B(4): 0.0	5.6
2020	PHI	MLB	29	560	104	30.1	.306	1.7	C 9, 1B 1	4.1

Philadelphia Phillies 2020

J.T. Realmuto, continued

Batted Ball Distribution

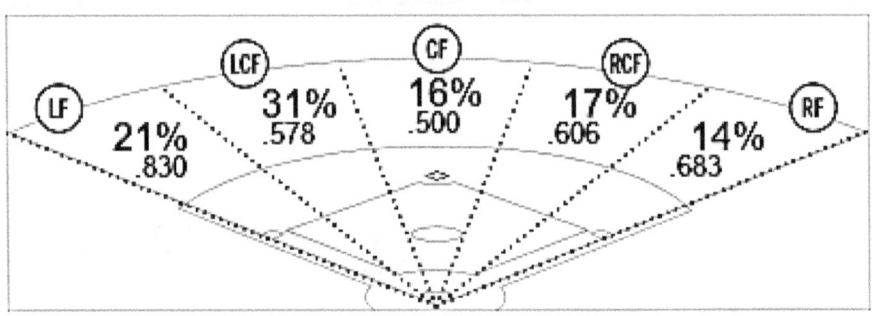

Strike Zone vs LHP   **Strike Zone vs RHP**

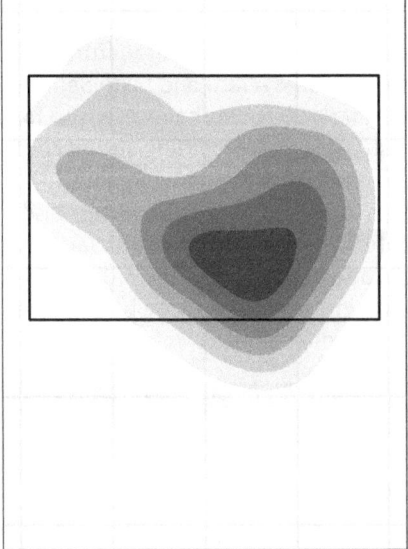

Jean Segura SS

Born: 03/17/90   Age: 30   Bats: R   Throws: R
Height: 5'10"   Weight: 205   Origin: International Free Agent, 2007

YEAR	TEAM	LVL	AGE	PA	R	2B	3B	HR	RBI	BB	K	SB	CS	AVG/OBP/SLG
2017	SEA	MLB	27	566	80	30	2	11	45	34	83	22	8	.300/.349/.427
2018	SEA	MLB	28	632	91	29	3	10	63	32	69	20	11	.304/.341/.415
2019	PHI	MLB	29	618	79	37	4	12	60	30	73	10	2	.280/.323/.420
2020	*PHI*	*MLB*	*30*	*595*	*59*	*31*	*3*	*12*	*62*	*30*	*83*	*20*	*7*	*.273/.317/.405*

Comparables: Angel Berroa, Jack Wilson, Elvis Andrus

In a year where balls flew out of the yard at a record pace, Segura slipped significantly by standing still. Never a patient hitter, Segura chased more offerings out of the zone while taking more pitches in it, which predictably led to poorer quality of contact and worse outcomes on balls in play. He also slipped defensively, although it was difficult to discern how much of this was Segura's fault as opposed to being a product of playing next to Maikel Franco and subsequently a parade of out-of-position third basemen. Always a durable player, Segura seemed to wear down as the season progressed, running less and losing what little power he had. He remains a decent enough option at short, but there's some risk the stagnation is real as he enters his 30s at a physically demanding position.

YEAR	TEAM	LVL	AGE	PA	DRC+	VORP	BABIP	BRR	FRAA	WARP
2017	SEA	MLB	27	566	104	27.4	.339	2.1	SS(124): -8.9	2.2
2018	SEA	MLB	28	632	105	35.5	.327	-1.0	SS(144): 3.4	3.5
2019	PHI	MLB	29	618	86	19.0	.302	2.5	SS(142): -3.8	1.7
2020	*PHI*	*MLB*	*30*	*595*	*90*	*16.7*	*.304*	*1.1*	*2B 0, SS -1*	*1.6*

Jean Segura, continued

Batted Ball Distribution

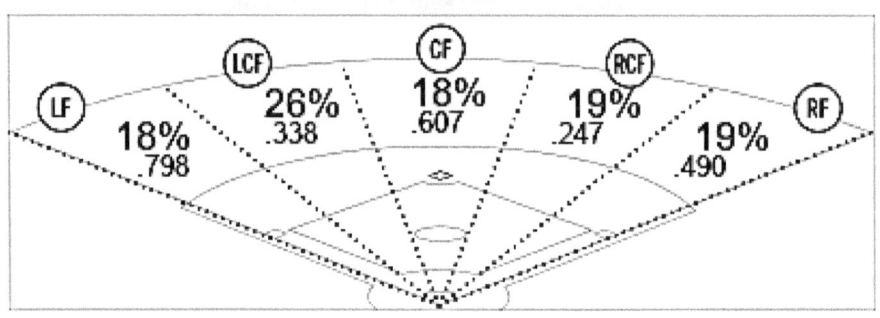

Strike Zone vs LHP   **Strike Zone vs RHP**

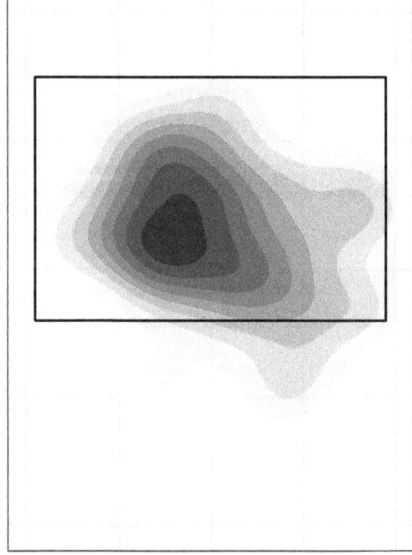

Neil Walker CI

Born: 09/10/85   Age: 34   Bats: B   Throws: R
Height: 6'3"   Weight: 210   Origin: Round 1, 2004 Draft (#11 overall)

YEAR	TEAM	LVL	AGE	PA	R	2B	3B	HR	RBI	BB	K	SB	CS	AVG/OBP/SLG
2017	NYN	MLB	31	299	40	13	2	10	36	27	47	0	1	.264/.339/.442
2017	MIL	MLB	31	149	19	8	0	4	13	28	30	0	1	.267/.409/.433
2018	NYA	MLB	32	398	48	12	1	11	46	42	87	0	0	.219/.309/.354
2019	MIA	MLB	33	381	37	19	1	8	38	42	77	3	0	.261/.344/.395
2020	MIA	MLB	34	251	26	9	1	6	26	25	54	1	1	.233/.317/.365

Comparables: Chase Utley, Gordon Beckham, Asdrúbal Cabrera

"There are four million different kinds of animals and plants in the world," says David Attenborough. "Four million different solutions to the problems of staying alive." In the ecosystem of Major League Baseball, some of these different plants and animals, and the solutions they represent, are dying at an alarming rate. Is the veteran, bench-bat utility infielder going extinct? One could ask Walker, who rebounded slightly in 2019 from an abysmal season in the Bronx, although the switch-hitting Pirates legend seems to have forgotten his power stroke even with the advent of the juiced ball. Walker surely ascribes to the Attenboroughian mantra, "even here, there is life"—as long as "life" means league-average hitting.

YEAR	TEAM	LVL	AGE	PA	DRC+	VORP	BABIP	BRR	FRAA	WARP
2017	NYN	MLB	31	299	107	12.3	.286	-1.5	2B(68): -5.0, 1B(3): 0.0	0.5
2017	MIL	MLB	31	149	108	9.7	.326	-0.7	2B(27): -1.1, 1B(14): 0.0	0.4
2018	NYA	MLB	32	398	89	-0.8	.257	-1.0	1B(42): 4.2, 2B(32): 0.7	0.7
2019	MIA	MLB	33	381	95	5.8	.316	-0.3	1B(69): -2.2, 3B(26): -2.5	0.1
2020	MIA	MLB	34	251	83	2.0	.280	-0.5	2B -1, 1B 1	0.1

Philadelphia Phillies 2020

Neil Walker, continued

Batted Ball Distribution

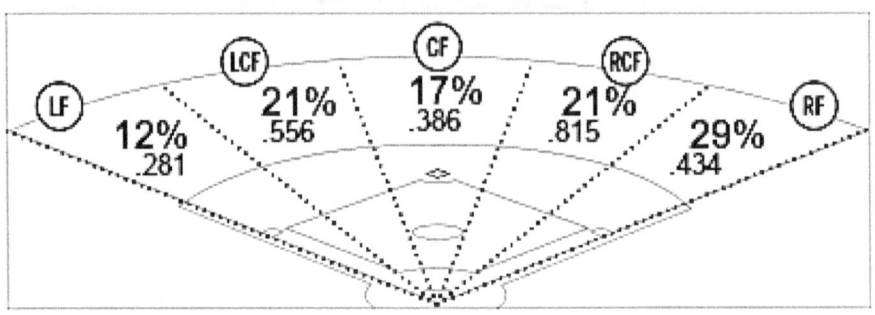

Strike Zone vs LHP   **Strike Zone vs RHP**

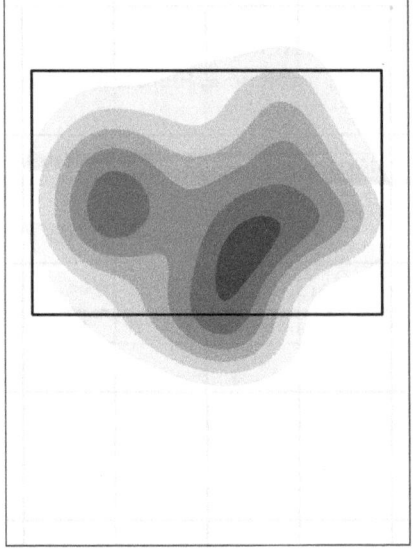

Nick Williams LF

Born: 09/08/93   Age: 26   Bats: L   Throws: L
Height: 6'3"   Weight: 195   Origin: Round 2, 2012 Draft (#93 overall)

YEAR	TEAM	LVL	AGE	PA	R	2B	3B	HR	RBI	BB	K	SB	CS	AVG/OBP/SLG
2017	LEH	AAA	23	306	43	16	2	15	44	16	90	5	4	.280/.328/.511
2017	PHI	MLB	23	343	45	14	4	12	55	20	97	1	2	.288/.338/.473
2018	PHI	MLB	24	448	53	12	3	17	50	32	111	3	2	.256/.324/.425
2019	LEH	AAA	25	210	33	15	2	10	25	14	52	1	0	.316/.381/.574
2019	PHI	MLB	25	112	9	4	0	2	5	4	43	0	0	.151/.196/.245
2020	PHI	MLB	26	98	11	4	1	4	13	5	30	1	1	.241/.294/.432

Comparables: Gus Bell, Justin Upton, Bob Chance

Buried on the bench after the Bryce Harper signing, Williams struggled in a pinch-hitting/reserve role and couldn't get back on track even when regular playing time briefly materialized. It didn't help that after injuries ravaged the outfield, Philadelphia acquired Jay Bruce and Corey Dickerson with no interest in granting Williams an extended opportunity. It's hard to blame the Phillies for looking for better options than a poor defensive corner outfielder with a career 96 DRC+ entering 2019. It's also understandable that a 25-year-old with strong prospect pedigree and no clear shot at playing time got frustrated and started hacking at everything thrown his way. Williams needs a change of scenery badly but might not be good enough to get the opportunity.

YEAR	TEAM	LVL	AGE	PA	DRC+	VORP	BABIP	BRR	FRAA	WARP
2017	LEH	AAA	23	306	120	14.0	.358	0.4	RF(37): 6.2, LF(17): 1.5	1.9
2017	PHI	MLB	23	343	93	18.5	.375	-0.8	RF(58): -5.9, CF(16): -2.0	-0.3
2018	PHI	MLB	24	448	98	11.4	.312	-1.4	RF(95): -9.8, LF(19): -1.5	-0.4
2019	LEH	AAA	25	210	130	17.4	.391	1.4	LF(20): 1.2, CF(16): 1.0	1.7
2019	PHI	MLB	25	112	45	-4.6	.230	0.4	LF(23): 0.0, RF(5): -0.3	-0.4
2020	PHI	MLB	26	98	87	1.1	.311	-0.1	LF 0, RF 0	0.1

Philadelphia Phillies 2020

Nick Williams, continued

Batted Ball Distribution

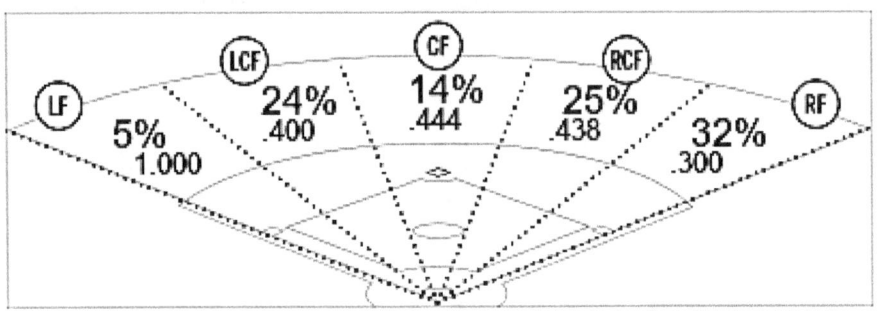

Strike Zone vs LHP   **Strike Zone vs RHP**

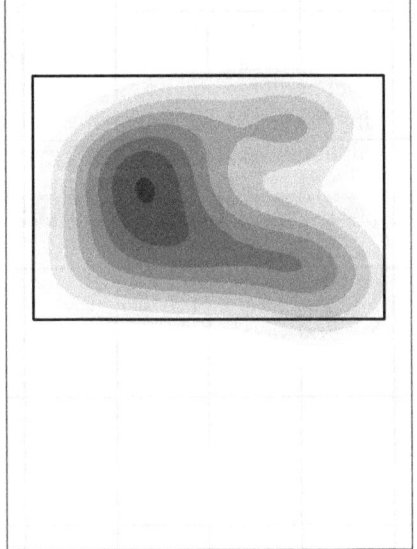

Jake Arrieta RHP

Born: 03/06/86   Age: 34   Bats: R   Throws: R
Height: 6'4"   Weight: 225   Origin: Round 5, 2007 Draft (#159 overall)

YEAR	TEAM	LVL	AGE	W	L	SV	G	GS	IP	H	HR	BB/9	K/9	K	GB%	BABIP
2017	CHN	MLB	31	14	10	0	30	30	168[1]	150	23	2.9	8.7	163	46%	.279
2018	PHI	MLB	32	10	11	0	31	31	172[2]	165	21	3.0	7.2	138	52%	.289
2019	PHI	MLB	33	8	8	0	24	24	135[2]	149	21	3.4	7.3	110	53%	.316
2020	PHI	MLB	34	8	9	0	24	24	136	144	22	3.4	7.5	114	52%	.302

Comparables: Ian Kennedy, Jeff Samardzija, Jason Schmidt

If the 2017-2018 version of Arrieta was him slowly backsliding from his 2015 Cy Young form, the 2019 version was Wily E. Coyote falling hundreds of miles into a desert ravine. As Arrieta ages and his velocity gradually declines, he has relied more and more on guile and location to get hitters out. It seemed to work for a while at the start of the season, when he posted a decent 3.60 ERA in his first 11 starts but didn't work so well in his final 13 starts, when he was pummeled to the tune of a ghastly 5.76 ERA. Arrieta's season was cut short in mid-August, and officially ended later that month when he had surgery to remove bone spurs from his elbow. To what degree the injury was the culprit for Arrieta's performance decline is an open question, but a healthy Arrieta is a much better bet for success than a cartoon coyote and a kilo of Acme dynamite.

YEAR	TEAM	LVL	AGE	WHIP	ERA	DRA	WARP	MPH	FB%	WHF	CSP
2017	CHN	MLB	31	1.22	3.53	4.09	2.8	94.1	64.3	9.3	49.1
2018	PHI	MLB	32	1.29	3.96	4.08	2.4	95.2	55.8	8.8	50.1
2019	PHI	MLB	33	1.47	4.64	5.45	0.5	94.6	56.2	7.9	46.9
2020	PHI	MLB	34	1.44	4.94	4.90	1.4	93.6	57.3	8.5	47.8

Jake Arrieta, continued

Pitch Shape vs LHH

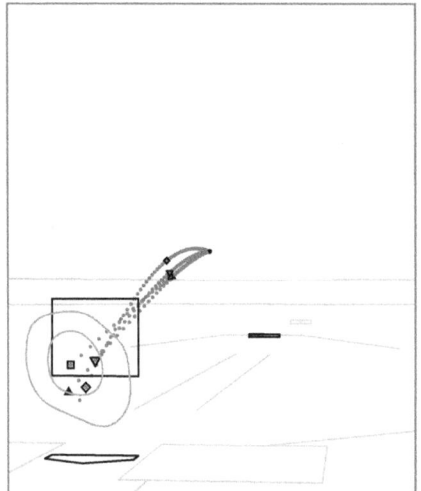

Pitch Shape vs RHH

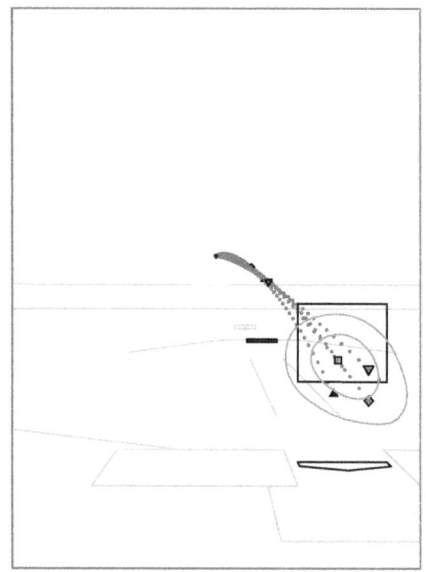

Type	Frequency	Velocity	H Movement	V Movement
● Fastball				
☐ Sinker	54.7%	92.9 [101]	-13.8 [92]	-20.4 [100]
+ Cutter				
▲ Changeup	18.3%	88 [110]	-14.3 [85]	-31.2 [89]
✕ Splitter				
▽ Slider	12.1%	90.2 [124]	3 [92]	-22.5 [131]
◇ Curveball	13.4%	81 [108]	12.5 [120]	-46.9 [101]
✤ Slow Curveball				
✱ Knuckleball				
▼ Screwball				

Seranthony Domínguez RHP

Born: 11/25/94 Age: 25 Bats: R Throws: R
Height: 6'1" Weight: 185 Origin: International Free Agent, 2011

YEAR	TEAM	LVL	AGE	W	L	SV	G	GS	IP	H	HR	BB/9	K/9	K	GB%	BABIP
2017	CLR	A+	22	4	4	0	15	13	62^1	51	6	4.3	10.8	75	45%	.306
2018	REA	AA	23	1	2	0	8	0	13	8	0	1.4	12.5	18	52%	.296
2018	PHI	MLB	23	2	5	16	53	0	58	32	4	3.4	11.5	74	56%	.220
2019	PHI	MLB	24	3	0	0	27	0	24^2	24	3	4.4	10.6	29	56%	.323
2020	PHI	MLB	25	2	2	3	42	0	44	36	6	4.1	11.3	56	52%	.287

Comparables: Trevor Rosenthal, Hansel Robles, Ryan Helsley

Pity the poor folks in any professional team's marketing department. Unless you're talking about a bonafide superstar, it's difficult to build a promotional campaign around any player thanks to performance variability and the risk of injury in any given season. One of the most electrifying non-closing relievers in baseball in 2018, Domínguez wasn't nearly as effective last year before being shut down in June with an elbow injury. A partial UCL tear was discovered, and the Phillies won't know until spring training if he will be healed enough to pitch or if surgery will be required. Cancel the Knights of the Round Table giveaway. Send back the foam promotional swords for Jousting Competition Day (for the first 5,000 fans ages 14 and under only, please). This Seranthony might not be taking to the field of battle anytime soon.

YEAR	TEAM	LVL	AGE	WHIP	ERA	DRA	WARP	MPH	FB%	WHF	CSP
2017	CLR	A+	22	1.30	3.61	4.59	0.5				
2018	REA	AA	23	0.77	2.08	1.65	0.5				
2018	PHI	MLB	23	0.93	2.95	3.00	1.3	99.7	66.6	16.3	49.1
2019	PHI	MLB	24	1.46	4.01	4.20	0.3	99.3	61.2	14.4	46.9
2020	PHI	MLB	25	1.25	3.48	3.53	0.9	99.3	66.1	16	49

Seranthony Domínguez, continued

Pitch Shape vs LHH

Pitch Shape vs RHH

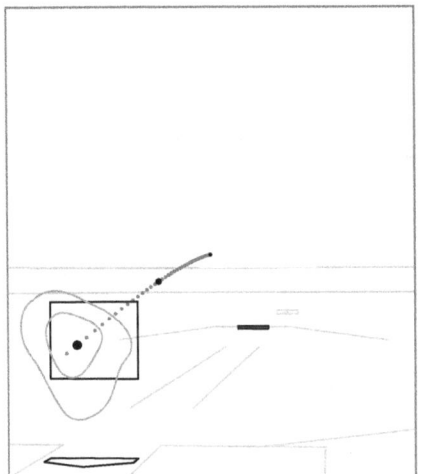
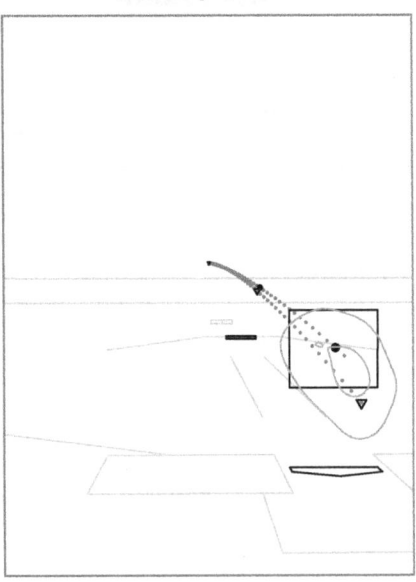

Type	Frequency	Velocity	H Movement	V Movement
● Fastball	59.7%	97.9 [116]	-1.5 [124]	-14.1 [105]
☐ Sinker				
+ Cutter				
▲ Changeup	4.7%	91.7 [123]	-12.9 [92]	-23.2 [112]
✕ Splitter				
▽ Slider	34.1%	90.1 [124]	4.4 [98]	-28.3 [114]
◇ Curveball				
⬥ Slow Curveball				
✱ Knuckleball				
▼ Screwball				

Zach Eflin RHP

Born: 04/08/94 Age: 26 Bats: R Throws: R
Height: 6'6" Weight: 215 Origin: Round 1, 2012 Draft (#33 overall)

YEAR	TEAM	LVL	AGE	W	L	SV	G	GS	IP	H	HR	BB/9	K/9	K	GB%	BABIP
2017	PHL	RK	23	0	0	0	2	2	7	5	0	0.0	7.7	6	55%	.250
2017	LEH	AAA	23	1	4	0	8	7	43¹	48	3	3.1	7.9	38	41%	.346
2017	PHI	MLB	23	1	5	0	11	11	64¹	79	16	1.7	4.9	35	46%	.297
2018	LEH	AAA	24	2	2	0	4	4	20	20	0	2.2	6.8	15	46%	.317
2018	PHI	MLB	24	11	8	0	24	24	128	130	16	2.6	8.6	123	43%	.309
2019	PHI	MLB	25	10	13	0	32	28	163¹	172	28	2.6	7.1	129	46%	.291
2020	PHI	MLB	26	7	9	0	24	24	134	147	26	2.8	7.4	110	44%	.303

Comparables: Jeanmar Gómez, Blake Beavan, Jake Thompson

To a casual fan there might not seem to be a reason for Eflin's perennial inconsistency. He'll have a great month where it looks like everything is coming together, the cutter morphing into a devastating pitch, a move to a different side of the rubber making him virtually unhittable. Then it will all come crumbing down, and Eflin will look like the extremely hittable pitcher he was in early July before the Phils banished him to the bullpen. The reality is Eflin has worked diligently to find the right combination of pitch types and location that work for him, but hitters keep successfully adapting to the changes. There will come a time where Eflin settles in as the pitcher he is, the results are more consistent, and he's a starting pitcher who capably fills out the back-end of a rotation.

YEAR	TEAM	LVL	AGE	WHIP	ERA	DRA	WARP	MPH	FB%	WHF	CSP
2017	PHL	RK	23	0.71	1.29	2.56	0.3				
2017	LEH	AAA	23	1.45	4.57	4.57	0.5				
2017	PHI	MLB	23	1.41	6.16	5.62	0.0	95.8	68.1	7.6	51
2018	LEH	AAA	24	1.25	4.05	4.38	0.3				
2018	PHI	MLB	24	1.30	4.36	4.67	1.0	96.9	58.2	11.5	51.4
2019	PHI	MLB	25	1.35	4.13	5.13	1.1	95.7	55.5	9.7	48.5
2020	PHI	MLB	26	1.41	5.17	5.13	1.1	95.7	59.1	10.2	51

Zach Eflin, continued

Pitch Shape vs LHH

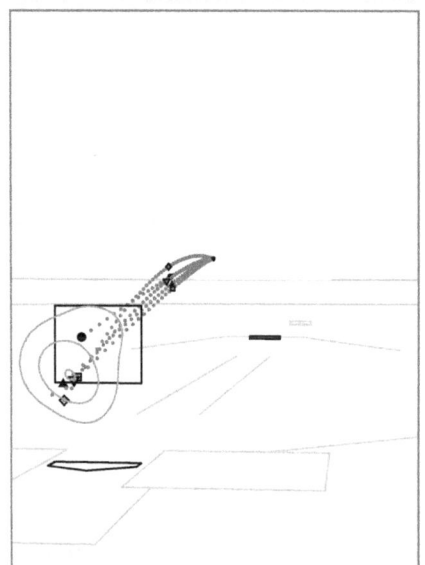

Pitch Shape vs RHH

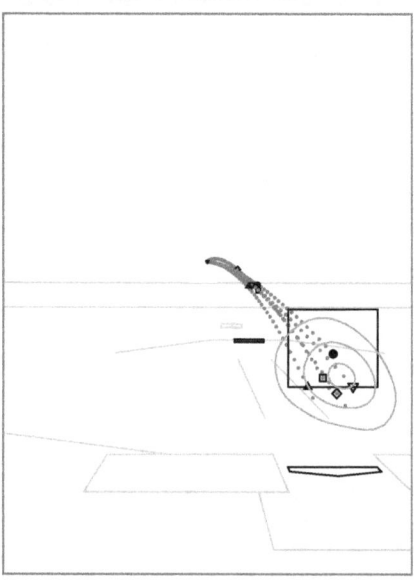

Type	Frequency	Velocity	H Movement	V Movement
● Fastball	33.3%	94.3 [105]	-7.8 [96]	-15.7 [101]
□ Sinker	22.2%	93.6 [105]	-14.1 [91]	-20.9 [98]
+ Cutter				
▲ Changeup	7.9%	87.1 [107]	-12.2 [95]	-25 [107]
✕ Splitter				
▽ Slider	30.7%	87.5 [113]	3.8 [95]	-26.1 [120]
◇ Curveball	5.4%	78.2 [99]	9.7 [109]	-46.4 [102]
⊕ Slow Curveball				
✳ Knuckleball				
▼ Screwball				

Francisco Liriano LHP

Born: 10/26/83 Age: 36 Bats: L Throws: L
Height: 6'3" Weight: 218 Origin: International Free Agent, 2000

YEAR	TEAM	LVL	AGE	W	L	SV	G	GS	IP	H	HR	BB/9	K/9	K	GB%	BABIP
2017	TOR	MLB	33	6	5	0	18	18	82^2	91	11	4.7	8.1	74	44%	.327
2017	HOU	MLB	33	0	2	0	20	0	14^1	14	0	6.3	6.9	11	54%	.341
2018	DET	MLB	34	5	12	0	27	26	133^2	127	19	4.9	7.4	110	49%	.285
2019	PIT	MLB	35	5	3	0	69	0	70	60	8	4.5	8.1	63	52%	.271
2020	*PIT*	*MLB*	*36*	*2*	*2*	*0*	*33*	*0*	*35*	*32*	*5*	*4.6*	*9.1*	*36*	*50%*	*.289*

Comparables: Jon Lester, Gio Gonzalez, Mark Langston

It didn't seem possible, but Liriano might have added a couple more years to his career by embracing the bullpen. Indeed, 2019 was the first time in his career he went an entire season without a start. His pitches had a skosh more zip, sure, and yet the real key to his success was avoiding all those mean right-handers: He faced lefties in 29 percent of his plate appearances, a new personal high. He also had the lowest BABIP of his long career—a career so long, in fact, he was once teammates with Terry freaking Mulholland. Liriano could probably use some pointers from Grandpa Terry, since that he was abysmal in back-to-back situations. If he can get that aspect figured out, though, he might pitch into his 40s, the way lefties were meant to.

YEAR	TEAM	LVL	AGE	WHIP	ERA	DRA	WARP	MPH	FB%	WHF	CSP
2017	TOR	MLB	33	1.62	5.88	5.75	-0.2	95.0	49.3	10.1	42.2
2017	HOU	MLB	33	1.67	4.40	6.59	-0.2	96.4	54.6	10	44
2018	DET	MLB	34	1.50	4.58	5.36	-0.1	94.4	46.7	10.5	43.8
2019	PIT	MLB	35	1.36	3.47	4.53	0.6	95.0	43.8	14.3	45.4
2020	*PIT*	*MLB*	*36*	*1.44*	*4.63*	*4.61*	*0.3*	*93.5*	*45.8*	*11.2*	*43.2*

Philadelphia Phillies 2020

Francisco Liriano, continued

Pitch Shape vs LHH   Pitch Shape vs RHH

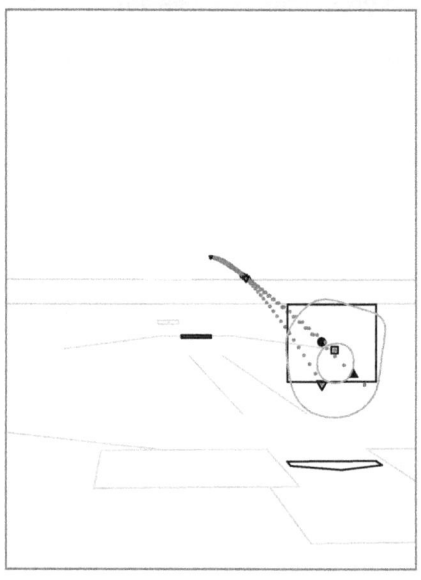

Type	Frequency	Velocity	H Movement	V Movement
● Fastball	6.6%	93.1 [102]	9.5 [88]	-15.8 [100]
☐ Sinker	37.2%	93.2 [103]	12.3 [102]	-18.3 [107]
✚ Cutter				
▲ Changeup	24.9%	87.2 [107]	13.2 [90]	-25.8 [105]
✕ Splitter				
▽ Slider	31.1%	87.4 [113]	-1.1 [84]	-26.3 [120]
◇ Curveball				
⊕ Slow Curveball				
✻ Knuckleball				
▼ Screwball				

Reggie McClain RHP

Born: 11/16/92   Age: 27   Bats: R   Throws: R
Height: 6'2"   Weight: 180   Origin: Round 13, 2016 Draft (#387 overall)

YEAR	TEAM	LVL	AGE	W	L	SV	G	GS	IP	H	HR	BB/9	K/9	K	GB%	BABIP
2017	MOD	A+	24	12	9	0	27	27	153^1	164	15	2.1	7.5	127	50%	.323
2018	MOD	A+	25	6	11	0	24	23	133	160	16	1.9	7.3	108	52%	.343
2019	MOD	A+	26	0	0	0	6	0	16	9	1	0.0	10.1	18	62%	.205
2019	ARK	AA	26	0	0	0	6	2	15^2	6	0	2.3	11.5	20	58%	.194
2019	TAC	AAA	26	3	4	2	17	1	41	29	3	4.0	7.5	34	58%	.241
2019	SEA	MLB	26	1	1	0	14	2	21	22	2	5.6	4.7	11	63%	.290
2020	*SEA*	*MLB*	*27*	*1*	*1*	*0*	*19*	*0*	*20*	*24*	*3*	*3.8*	*6.0*	*13*	*58%*	*.316*

Comparables: Joe Martinez, Cole Sulser, Jeff Brigham

McClain is the kind of new-age player dev success story that the best teams seem to replicate so frequently. After two straight nondescript years as an old-for-the-level college pitcher in the California League, he attended the Mariners' offseason "Gas Camp," where he saw his velocity and big-league prospects spike beyond what previously seemed possible. The third time was the charm for McClain in the Cal League—this time, as a reliever—where he dominated in six April appearances, kick-starting a race through the system that landed him in the Mariners bullpen come August. Eleven of those 14 earned runs came against the Astros, in Houston, across three appearances, one of which was his big-league debut. What happened to cracking down on rookie hazing?

YEAR	TEAM	LVL	AGE	WHIP	ERA	DRA	WARP	MPH	FB%	WHF	CSP
2017	MOD	A+	24	1.30	4.75	4.76	0.9				
2018	MOD	A+	25	1.41	5.01	6.41	-1.7				
2019	MOD	A+	26	0.56	0.56	1.52	0.6				
2019	ARK	AA	26	0.64	1.15	2.25	0.5				
2019	TAC	AAA	26	1.15	3.29	2.28	1.6				
2019	SEA	MLB	26	1.67	6.00	6.78	-0.3	96.4	76.6	6.8	47.6
2020	*SEA*	*MLB*	*27*	*1.62*	*6.01*	*5.68*	*-0.1*	*95.9*	*77.5*	*6.9*	*48.2*

Reggie McClain, continued

Pitch Shape vs LHH	Pitch Shape vs RHH
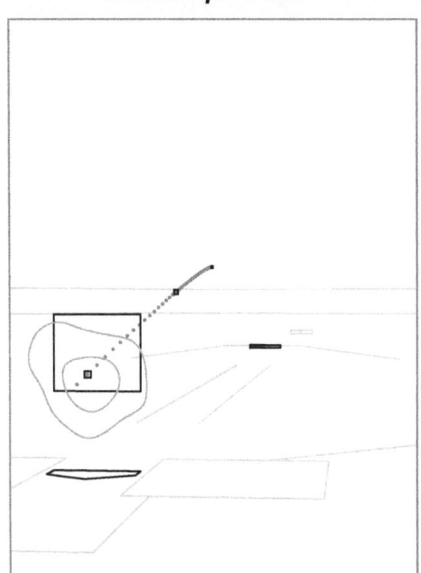	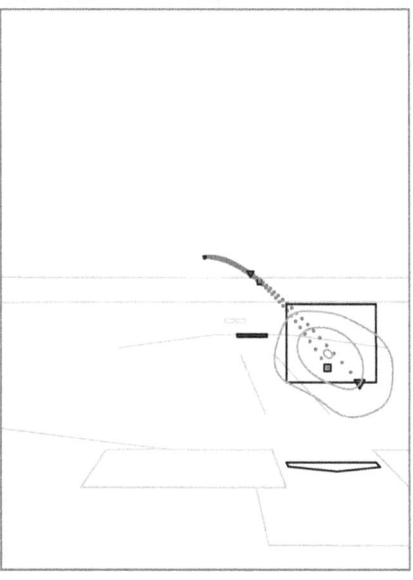

Type	Frequency	Velocity	H Movement	V Movement
● Fastball	9.3%	94.4 [106]	-14.4 [66]	-19.8 [90]
☐ Sinker	67.2%	93.9 [107]	-15.5 [81]	-22.7 [92]
+ Cutter				
▲ Changeup	5.4%	88.3 [111]	-14 [87]	-23.9 [110]
✕ Splitter				
▽ Slider	18.1%	84.1 [99]	1 [83]	-34 [97]
◇ Curveball				
✜ Slow Curveball				
✳ Knuckleball				
▼ Screwball				

Adam Morgan   LHP

Born: 02/27/90   Age: 30   Bats: L   Throws: L
Height: 6'1"   Weight: 200   Origin: Round 3, 2011 Draft (#120 overall)

YEAR	TEAM	LVL	AGE	W	L	SV	G	GS	IP	H	HR	BB/9	K/9	K	GB%	BABIP
2017	LEH	AAA	27	0	1	0	12	0	17^1	19	1	2.6	7.3	14	44%	.340
2017	PHI	MLB	27	3	3	0	37	0	54^2	51	10	3.0	10.4	63	45%	.297
2018	PHI	MLB	28	0	2	1	67	0	49^1	49	5	4.0	9.1	50	54%	.324
2019	PHI	MLB	29	3	3	0	40	0	29^2	20	4	3.0	8.8	29	41%	.216
2020	*PHI*	*MLB*	*30*	*2*	*2*	*3*	*37*	*0*	*39*	*37*	*6*	*2.9*	*9.5*	*41*	*44%*	*.293*

Comparables: T.J. McFarland, Vidal Nuño III, TJ House

Morgan's career has seen more second acts than the Off-Broadway production of The Fantasticks. The most recent incarnation of Morgan featured less velocity and fewer fastballs than ever, with more curves and changes supplementing a devastating slider. Morgan was effective across the board, but his best work came against his fellow southpaws, who struck out frequently and mostly generated weak contact on those rare occasions when they did put lumber on the ball. Injuries derailed Morgan's season; he tried pitching through a flexor strain in his elbow but was shut down in early August after posting a 7.15 ERA in his final 16 appearances. The injury didn't require surgery, and Morgan is on track to be ready for spring training.

YEAR	TEAM	LVL	AGE	WHIP	ERA	DRA	WARP	MPH	FB%	WHF	CSP
2017	LEH	AAA	27	1.38	4.67	4.25	0.2				
2017	PHI	MLB	27	1.26	4.12	3.12	1.2	96.9	33.2	17.5	44.8
2018	PHI	MLB	28	1.44	3.83	4.31	0.4	96.2	34.9	13.1	48.5
2019	PHI	MLB	29	1.01	3.94	4.26	0.4	94.8	28.1	16.6	47
2020	*PHI*	*MLB*	*30*	*1.26*	*4.10*	*4.18*	*0.5*	*95.2*	*32.4*	*15.4*	*46.8*

Adam Morgan, continued

Pitch Shape vs LHH

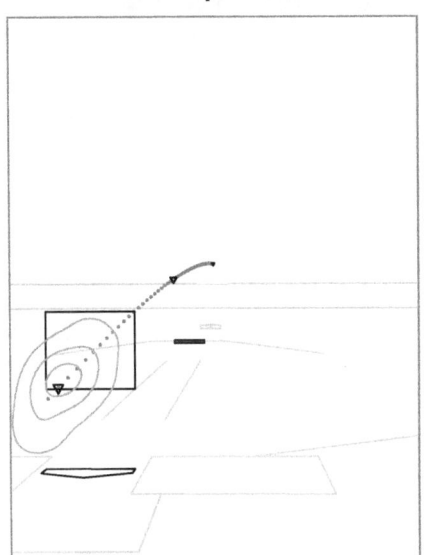

Pitch Shape vs RHH

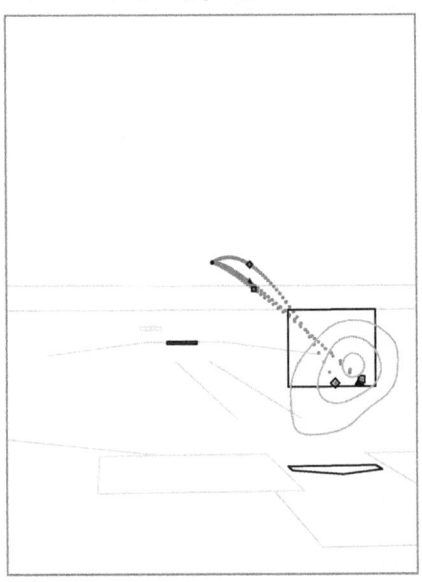

Type	Frequency	Velocity	H Movement	V Movement
● Fastball	6.9%	93.1 [102]	10.2 [85]	-15.5 [101]
☐ Sinker	21.2%	92.8 [101]	15.2 [84]	-20.7 [99]
+ Cutter				
▲ Changeup	20.3%	83.8 [95]	11.8 [97]	-26.8 [102]
✕ Splitter				
▽ Slider	37.4%	81.6 [88]	-9.2 [117]	-33.6 [99]
◇ Curveball	14.3%	77.6 [97]	-7.9 [102]	-48.1 [99]
⊕ Slow Curveball				
✱ Knuckleball				
▼ Screwball				

Héctor Neris RHP

Born: 06/14/89 Age: 31 Bats: R Throws: R
Height: 6'2" Weight: 215 Origin: International Free Agent, 2010

YEAR	TEAM	LVL	AGE	W	L	SV	G	GS	IP	H	HR	BB/9	K/9	K	GB%	BABIP
2017	PHI	MLB	28	4	5	26	74	0	74²	68	9	3.1	10.4	86	35%	.306
2018	LEH	AAA	29	2	0	1	19	0	18²	9	0	3.4	14.9	31	46%	.257
2018	PHI	MLB	29	1	3	11	53	0	47²	46	11	3.0	14.3	76	33%	.354
2019	PHI	MLB	30	3	6	28	68	0	67²	45	10	3.2	11.8	89	46%	.240
2020	PHI	MLB	31	3	3	32	53	0	56	44	8	4.2	12.7	79	42%	.297

Comparables: Erik Goeddel, Vinnie Pestano, Jacob Barnes

Few pitchers use a split-fingered fastball anymore, but in a world that has gone gluten free Neris' splitter is his bread-and-butter; he used it 67 percent of the time, far more than anyone else. Neris' big hands and thick, elongated fingers give him the unique ability to command a pitch that for most hurlers darts toward home plate with little if any precision. Neris has a solid fastball he can dial up to 95 mph, but it is his mastery of the splitter and ability to throw it for strikes when needed that makes him an asset. He is prone to the long ball when his signature pitch doesn't work, but Neris' one great skill has quietly made him one of the better relievers in the game.

YEAR	TEAM	LVL	AGE	WHIP	ERA	DRA	WARP	MPH	FB%	WHF	CSP
2017	PHI	MLB	28	1.26	3.01	4.25	0.8	96.2	48.6	17.8	48.3
2018	LEH	AAA	29	0.86	1.45	1.86	0.7				
2018	PHI	MLB	29	1.30	5.10	2.36	1.4	97.0	47.1	20.5	46.5
2019	PHI	MLB	30	1.02	2.93	2.92	1.8	96.1	34.5	18.8	38.8
2020	PHI	MLB	31	1.25	3.73	3.75	1.0	95.5	41.7	18.8	43.4

Philadelphia Phillies 2020

Héctor Neris, continued

Pitch Shape vs LHH

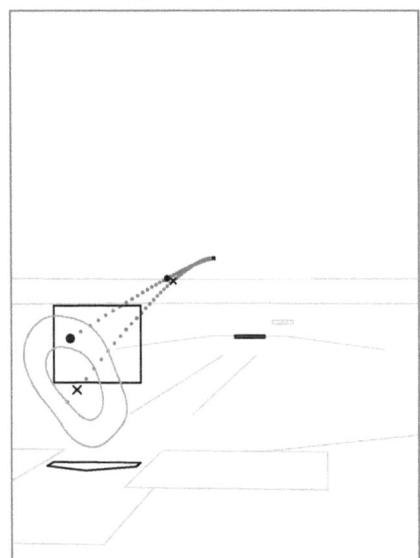

Pitch Shape vs RHH

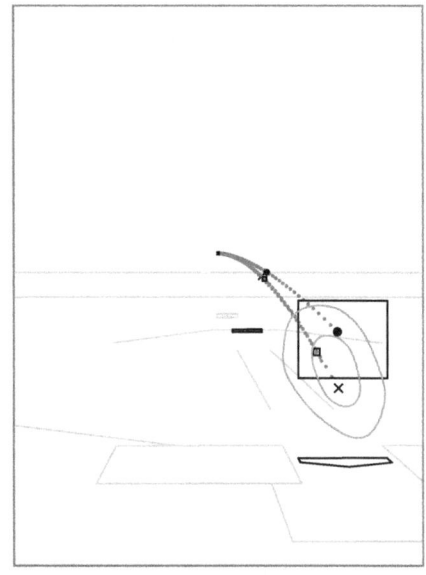

Type	Frequency	Velocity	H Movement	V Movement
● Fastball	26.8%	94.8 [107]	-8.2 [94]	-13.9 [105]
☐ Sinker	7.8%	95.2 [113]	-14.1 [90]	-19 [105]
+ Cutter				
▲ Changeup				
✕ Splitter	65.5%	87.3 [110]	-6.3 [106]	-31.5 [92]
▽ Slider				
◇ Curveball				
✥ Slow Curveball				
✱ Knuckleball				
▼ Screwball				

Aaron Nola RHP

Born: 06/04/93 Age: 27 Bats: R Throws: R
Height: 6'2" Weight: 195 Origin: Round 1, 2014 Draft (#7 overall)

YEAR	TEAM	LVL	AGE	W	L	SV	G	GS	IP	H	HR	BB/9	K/9	K	GB%	BABIP
2017	LEH	AAA	24	1	0	0	2	2	10^1	6	0	0.9	8.7	10	65%	.231
2017	PHI	MLB	24	12	11	0	27	27	168	154	18	2.6	9.9	184	50%	.309
2018	PHI	MLB	25	17	6	0	33	33	212^1	149	17	2.5	9.5	224	52%	.251
2019	PHI	MLB	26	12	7	0	34	34	202^1	176	27	3.6	10.2	229	51%	.295
2020	PHI	MLB	27	11	9	0	29	29	172	153	22	3.3	10.1	194	51%	.298

Comparables: Gerrit Cole, Tommy Hanson, Luis Severino

It is a difficult feat to be a great player and fly under the proverbial radar, yet somehow Nola has managed to perform this magic trick with ease. Nola has been the seventh-best pitcher by WARP since 2016, yet inexplicably is a national nonentity. Even in Philadelphia, a city obsessed with its athletes to an unhealthy degree, Nola is frequently overlooked and overshadowed by more colorful superstars like Joel Embiid, Ben Simmons, Carson Wentz and teammate Bryce Harper. You can tick off all the obvious reasons: Nola's DRA is prettier than his ERA, he hasn't won a Cy Young award, has appeared in only one All-Star Game and hasn't tossed an inning in the playoffs. But most of this relative anonymity is because of the man himself. Nola is an unassuming athlete who goes about his business and stays off the back pages in a town where the media guzzles down controversy like a dog lapping up water on a scorching August afternoon. Locked up to a team-friendly contract through at least 2022, Nola is one of the most important components to the Phillies' present and future success.

YEAR	TEAM	LVL	AGE	WHIP	ERA	DRA	WARP	MPH	FB%	WHF	CSP
2017	LEH	AAA	24	0.68	0.87	1.89	0.4				
2017	PHI	MLB	24	1.21	3.54	3.22	4.4	94.4	53.3	11.8	49.1
2018	PHI	MLB	25	0.97	2.37	2.60	6.6	94.9	49.5	13.1	48.4
2019	PHI	MLB	26	1.27	3.87	3.46	5.1	95.3	46.2	11.8	44.7
2020	PHI	MLB	27	1.25	3.67	3.75	3.9	94.5	49.4	12.4	47.6

Aaron Nola, continued

Pitch Shape vs LHH

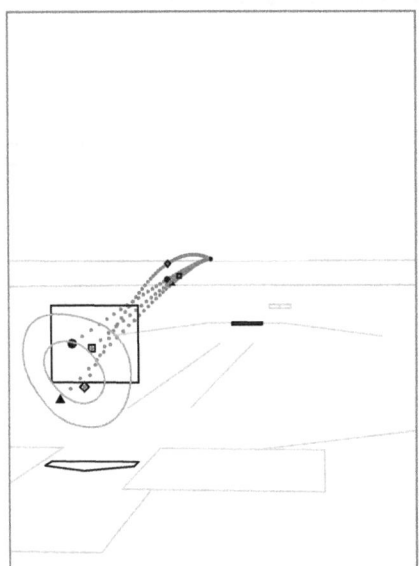

Pitch Shape vs RHH

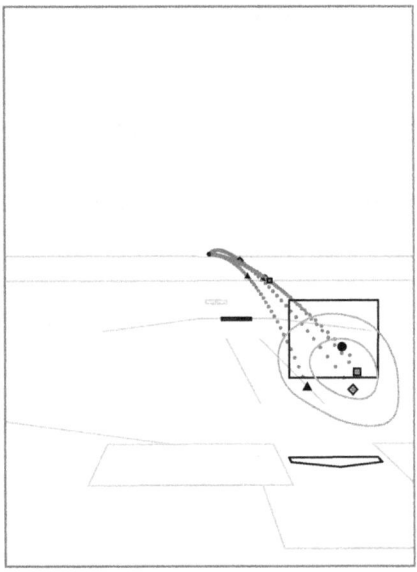

Type	Frequency	Velocity	H Movement	V Movement
● Fastball	34.1%	93.6 [103]	-11.2 [81]	-16.1 [99]
□ Sinker	12.1%	92.6 [100]	-14.5 [88]	-21.3 [97]
+ Cutter				
▲ Changeup	18.6%	86.2 [104]	-12.9 [92]	-29.5 [94]
✕ Splitter				
▽ Slider				
◇ Curveball	35.2%	79.5 [103]	13.7 [125]	-48.7 [98]
✦ Slow Curveball				
✱ Knuckleball				
▼ Screwball				

Blake Parker RHP

Born: 06/19/85 Age: 35 Bats: R Throws: R
Height: 6'3" Weight: 225 Origin: Round 16, 2006 Draft (#479 overall)

YEAR	TEAM	LVL	AGE	W	L	SV	G	GS	IP	H	HR	BB/9	K/9	K	GB%	BABIP
2017	LAA	MLB	32	3	3	8	71	0	67¹	40	7	2.1	11.5	86	48%	.229
2018	LAA	MLB	33	2	1	14	67	0	66¹	63	12	2.6	9.5	70	35%	.297
2019	PHI	MLB	34	2	1	0	23	2	25	19	6	2.2	11.2	31	32%	.241
2019	MIN	MLB	34	1	2	10	37	0	36¹	34	7	4.0	8.4	34	45%	.276
2020	PHI	MLB	35	2	2	0	33	0	35	31	6	3.2	9.5	37	40%	.280

Comparables: Shawn Kelley, Chris Schroder, Fernando Salas

Parker is a rare member of a dying breed: a pitcher who relies on a split-fingered fastball as either his primary or secondary pitch. Parker's splitter is the slowest in the game, averaging under 80 miles-per-hour. Velocity isn't everything, but with Parker's fastball dropping a couple of ticks since his career year in 2017, if his splitter doesn't have enough bite and drop, it flies out of the park with ease. Parker started the year as Minnesota's closer, but by July was designated for assignment as the Twins looked to younger and harder throwing arms. He was fine for the Phillies in August, but the NL caught up to him quickly down the stretch and he gave up runs in six of his 11 September appearances. Parker is a useful middle relief cog, but the line between useful reliever and former major leaguer gets finer with each passing year.

YEAR	TEAM	LVL	AGE	WHIP	ERA	DRA	WARP	MPH	FB%	WHF	CSP
2017	LAA	MLB	32	0.83	2.54	2.26	2.2	95.5	60	15.1	44.7
2018	LAA	MLB	33	1.24	3.26	5.19	-0.2	94.5	57.5	11.6	46.5
2019	PHI	MLB	34	1.00	5.04	2.97	0.7	92.3	46.9	12.9	45.6
2019	MIN	MLB	34	1.38	4.21	5.29	0.0	93.4	46.9	11.4	44.6
2020	PHI	MLB	35	1.26	4.09	4.27	0.4	92.9	52.9	12.4	44.6

Philadelphia Phillies 2020

Blake Parker, continued

Pitch Shape vs LHH

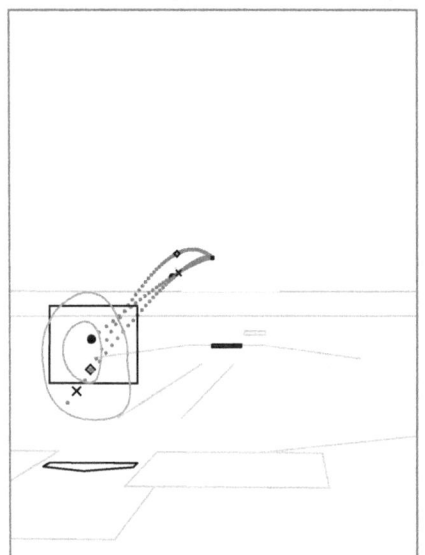

Pitch Shape vs RHH

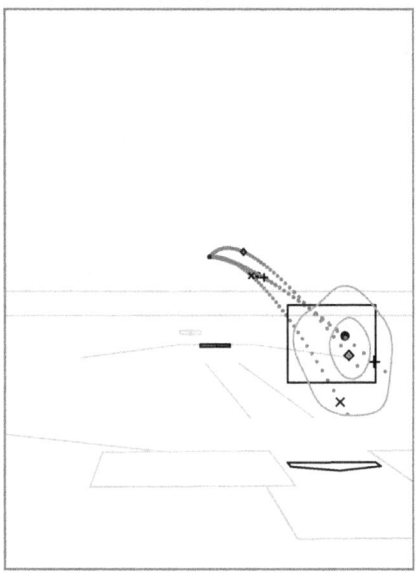

Type	Frequency	Velocity	H Movement	V Movement
● Fastball	47.9%	91.7 [98]	-2.2 [121]	-14.7 [103]
☐ Sinker				
+ Cutter	4.7%	88.5 [99]	2.7 [105]	-24.3 [99]
▲ Changeup				
✕ Splitter	32.3%	80.3 [79]	-7.6 [101]	-36.4 [76]
▽ Slider				
◇ Curveball	15.1%	76.4 [93]	7.1 [99]	-52.6 [89]
⬥ Slow Curveball				
✴ Knuckleball				
▼ Screwball				

Nick Pivetta   RHP

Born: 02/14/93   Age: 27   Bats: R   Throws: R
Height: 6'5"   Weight: 220   Origin: Round 4, 2013 Draft (#136 overall)

YEAR	TEAM	LVL	AGE	W	L	SV	G	GS	IP	H	HR	BB/9	K/9	K	GB%	BABIP
2017	LEH	AAA	24	5	0	0	5	5	32	25	1	0.6	10.4	37	40%	.293
2017	PHI	MLB	24	8	10	0	26	26	133	144	25	3.9	9.5	140	45%	.332
2018	PHI	MLB	25	7	14	0	33	32	164	163	24	2.8	10.3	188	50%	.327
2019	LEH	AAA	26	5	1	0	9	6	41	23	2	4.8	12.7	58	52%	.253
2019	PHI	MLB	26	4	6	1	30	13	93^2	103	20	3.7	8.6	89	45%	.309
2020	PHI	MLB	27	3	4	0	47	5	66	67	12	3.8	9.0	67	46%	.303

Comparables: Jerad Eickhoff, Domingo Germán, Jakob Junis

Some buzzwords get bandied about so frequently they lose all meaning. Pivetta was rightfully praised in 2018 for picking up a new and improved curveball with an elite spin rate, but there was little else in his profile to support the notion that 2019 would be a big step forward. In hindsight, we should have seen the struggles Pivetta endured coming from a million miles away. He consistently dials his heater up into the mid-90s, but the pitch is too straight and too ordinary of an offering to fool most hitters. Pivetta tried all sorts of things to remedy this shortcoming—throwing more off-speed stuff early in the year and then throwing harder late in the season—but hitters adapted faster than the Borg to a gaggle of non-Enterprise Starfleet officers. Maybe there's something else Pivetta can try, but until he develops a third pitch, it matters very little how much spin his curveball has.

YEAR	TEAM	LVL	AGE	WHIP	ERA	DRA	WARP	MPH	FB%	WHF	CSP
2017	LEH	AAA	24	0.84	1.41	2.03	1.3				
2017	PHI	MLB	24	1.51	6.02	4.66	1.4	96.8	66	10.1	50.2
2018	PHI	MLB	25	1.30	4.77	3.40	3.6	97.1	59	13.2	49.1
2019	LEH	AAA	26	1.10	3.07	1.99	1.9				
2019	PHI	MLB	26	1.52	5.38	5.07	0.6	97.0	51.1	11.3	48.8
2020	PHI	MLB	27	1.43	4.96	4.88	0.5	96.5	59.2	11.9	49.8

Nick Pivetta, continued

Pitch Shape vs LHH	Pitch Shape vs RHH
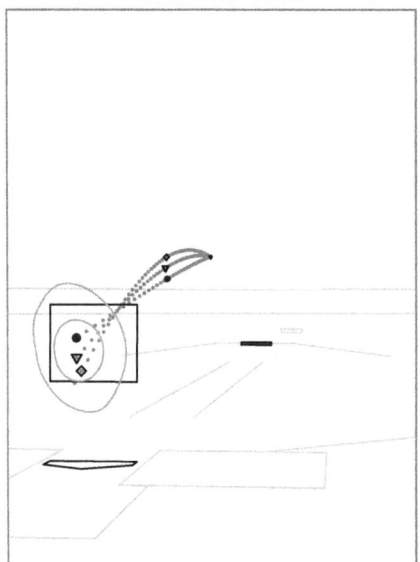	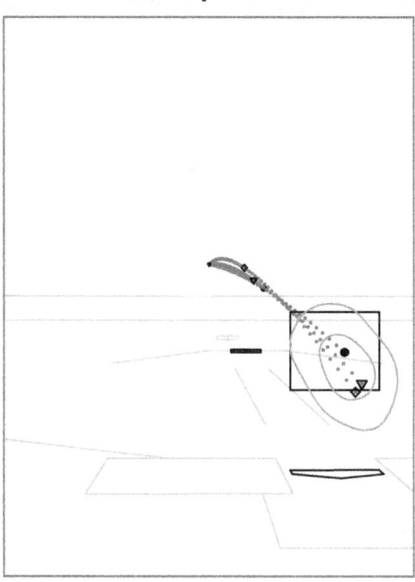

Type	Frequency	Velocity	H Movement	V Movement
● Fastball	49.0%	95 [107]	-8.3 [93]	-11.4 [112]
☐ Sinker				
+ Cutter				
▲ Changeup				
✕ Splitter				
▽ Slider	11.9%	86 [107]	4.7 [99]	-32.2 [103]
◇ Curveball	35.3%	80.8 [107]	10.9 [114]	-52.1 [90]
✦ Slow Curveball				
✱ Knuckleball				
▼ Screwball				

David Robertson RHP

Born: 04/09/85   Age: 35   Bats: R   Throws: R
Height: 5'11"   Weight: 195   Origin: Round 17, 2006 Draft (#524 overall)

YEAR	TEAM	LVL	AGE	W	L	SV	G	GS	IP	H	HR	BB/9	K/9	K	GB%	BABIP
2017	CHA	MLB	32	4	2	13	31	0	33^1	21	4	3.0	12.7	47	43%	.250
2017	NYA	MLB	32	5	0	1	30	0	35	14	2	3.1	13.1	51	56%	.182
2018	NYA	MLB	33	8	3	5	69	0	69^2	46	7	3.4	11.8	91	47%	.245
2019	PHI	MLB	34	0	1	0	7	0	6^2	8	1	8.1	8.1	6	33%	.350
2020	*PHI*	*MLB*	*35*	*2*	*2*	*0*	*33*	*0*	*35*	*30*	*6*	*3.7*	*11.1*	*43*	*43%*	*.292*

Comparables: Francisco Rodríguez, Greg Holland, Billy Wagner

Enlightened baseball fans in the 21st century don't care how much baseball players are paid by billionaire owners who could double their teams' payrolls and still have plenty to spare for a shiny, gold-plated yacht. On the other hand, TWO YEARS AND $23 MILLION FOR 6 2/3 INNINGS OF DAVID ROBERTSON? WHAT THE HELL? Advertised in the offseason as the lynchpin of the Phillies new-and-improved bullpen, Robertson made it as far as April 15 before being placed on the IL with elbow soreness. If you've followed baseball for any appreciable amount of time you know how this story usually ends. A flexor strain was discovered, a rehab attempt failed and Tommy John surgery in August knocked Robertson out of commission until 2021. It's a virtual impossibility the Phillies pick up their club option. D-Rob, we hardly knew ye.

YEAR	TEAM	LVL	AGE	WHIP	ERA	DRA	WARP	MPH	FB%	WHF	CSP
2017	CHA	MLB	32	0.96	2.70	1.98	1.2	93.6	56.1	16.5	46.9
2017	NYA	MLB	32	0.74	1.03	1.86	1.3	93.6	56.1	18.4	43.2
2018	NYA	MLB	33	1.03	3.23	3.03	1.5	94.5	42.5	14.4	43.3
2019	PHI	MLB	34	2.10	5.40	7.03	-0.1	94.1	57.4	11	42.7
2020	*PHI*	*MLB*	*35*	*1.28*	*4.04*	*4.10*	*0.5*	*92.9*	*47.8*	*14.9*	*42.7*

Philadelphia Phillies 2020

David Robertson, continued

Pitch Shape vs LHH

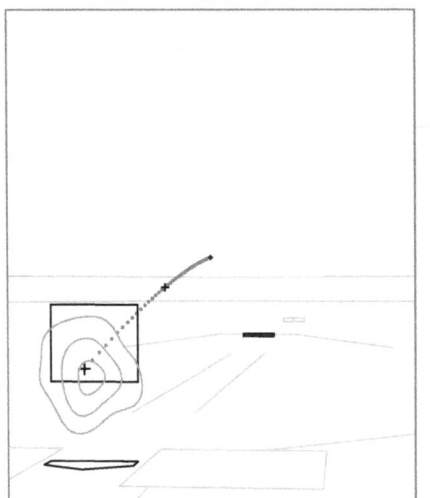

Pitch Shape vs RHH

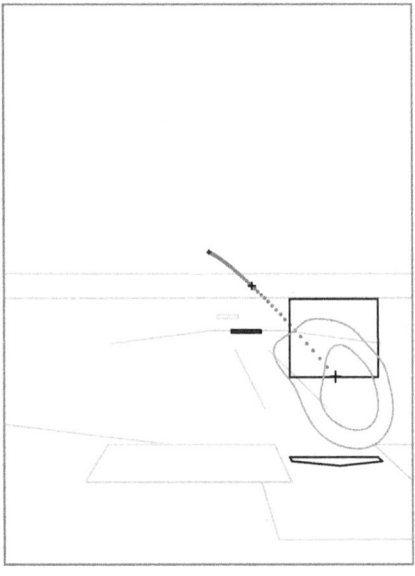

Type	Frequency	Velocity	H Movement	V Movement
● Fastball				
□ Sinker	4.4%	92.8 [101]	-7.6 [132]	-14.4 [121]
+ Cutter	52.9%	92.3 [123]	2.2 [102]	-13.9 [138]
▲ Changeup				
× Splitter				
▽ Slider	12.5%	87.3 [112]	6 [104]	-28.5 [113]
◇ Curveball	30.1%	83.2 [115]	9.5 [108]	-43.7 [108]
⊕ Slow Curveball				
✳ Knuckleball				
▼ Screwball				

Ranger Suárez LHP

Born: 08/26/95   Age: 24   Bats: L   Throws: L
Height: 6'1"   Weight: 180   Origin: International Free Agent, 2012

YEAR	TEAM	LVL	AGE	W	L	SV	G	GS	IP	H	HR	BB/9	K/9	K	GB%	BABIP
2017	LWD	A	21	6	2	0	14	14	85	52	4	2.5	9.5	90	58%	.233
2017	CLR	A+	21	2	4	0	8	8	37²	43	1	2.6	9.1	38	50%	.382
2018	REA	AA	22	4	3	0	12	12	75	64	2	2.4	6.5	54	51%	.283
2018	LEH	AAA	22	2	0	0	9	9	49¹	48	2	2.7	5.7	31	50%	.297
2018	PHI	MLB	22	1	1	0	4	3	15	21	3	3.6	6.6	11	52%	.367
2019	LEH	AAA	23	2	2	0	7	7	38	41	8	2.4	7.6	32	54%	.306
2019	PHI	MLB	23	6	1	0	37	0	48²	52	6	2.2	7.8	42	57%	.319
2020	PHI	MLB	24	2	2	0	42	0	44	48	7	3.1	7.1	35	53%	.304

Comparables: Devin Smeltzer, Reynaldo López, Derek Holland

"Ranger Suárez" sounds like a weird, long forgotten spin-off to Chuck Norris' television drama smash hit *Walker, Texas Ranger*, not a Phillies pitching prospect who got his first significant taste of big-league action in 2019. Suárez didn't kick ass the way Norris did in his seminal 1990s CBS vehicle, but was effective, using a four-pitch mix that kept hitters off balance even though he didn't dial up his velocity in relief as anticipated. Suárez could arguably but use more seasoning, but sometimes you must rise to the challenge and defeat whatever is thrown your way, whether you're pitching in middle relief for the Phillies on a sweltering August day or thwarting a group of international terrorists who have traveled to Texas to stop a peace conference that could finally unify the Balkans.

YEAR	TEAM	LVL	AGE	WHIP	ERA	DRA	WARP	MPH	FB%	WHF	CSP
2017	LWD	A	21	0.89	1.59	2.96	2.3				
2017	CLR	A+	21	1.43	3.82	5.54	-0.1				
2018	REA	AA	22	1.12	2.76	3.38	1.7				
2018	LEH	AAA	22	1.28	2.74	4.87	0.4				
2018	PHI	MLB	22	1.80	5.40	5.73	-0.1	94.1	60.4	7.6	51.1
2019	LEH	AAA	23	1.34	5.68	5.10	0.6				
2019	PHI	MLB	23	1.32	3.14	4.21	0.6	94.3	52.6	10.2	43.6
2020	PHI	MLB	24	1.42	4.79	4.75	0.3	94.1	55.7	10	48.4

Ranger Suárez, continued

Pitch Shape vs LHH

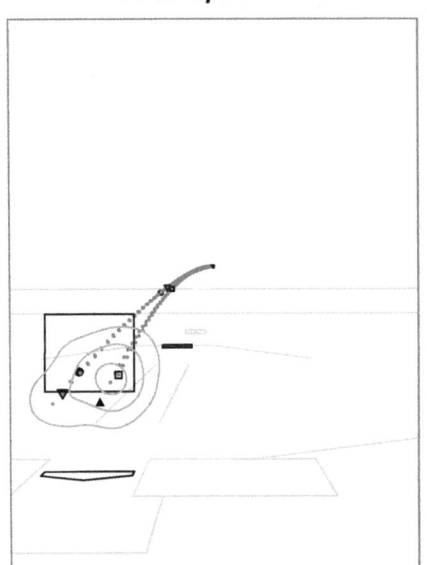

Pitch Shape vs RHH

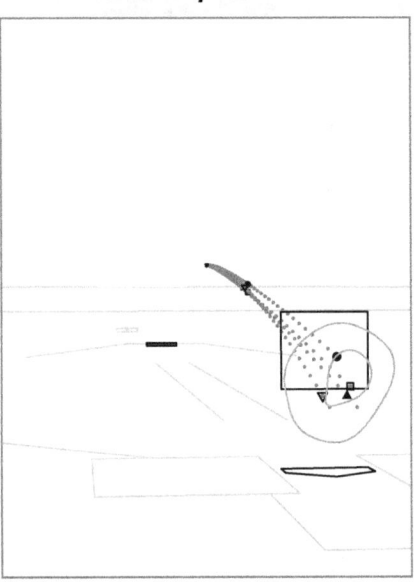

Type	Frequency	Velocity	H Movement	V Movement
● Fastball	23.8%	93.1 [102]	5.6 [106]	-18.6 [93]
☐ Sinker	28.9%	92.2 [98]	13.7 [93]	-22.6 [92]
+ Cutter				
▲ Changeup	26.8%	85.1 [99]	13.1 [91]	-28.6 [96]
✕ Splitter				
▽ Slider	20.6%	85.1 [103]	-2.6 [90]	-30.2 [108]
◇ Curveball				
⊕ Slow Curveball				
✱ Knuckleball				
▼ Screwball				

Anthony Swarzak RHP
Born: 09/10/85 Age: 34 Bats: R Throws: R
Height: 6'4" Weight: 215 Origin: Round 2, 2004 Draft (#61 overall)

YEAR	TEAM	LVL	AGE	W	L	SV	G	GS	IP	H	HR	BB/9	K/9	K	GB%	BABIP
2017	CHA	MLB	31	4	3	1	41	0	48^1	37	2	2.4	9.7	52	40%	.294
2017	MIL	MLB	31	2	1	1	29	0	29	21	4	2.8	12.1	39	51%	.270
2018	NYN	MLB	32	0	2	4	29	0	26^1	28	6	4.8	10.6	31	31%	.344
2019	ATL	MLB	33	1	2	1	44	0	39^2	38	6	4.3	7.9	35	49%	.291
2019	SEA	MLB	33	2	2	3	15	0	13^2	14	6	5.3	11.2	17	44%	.242
2020	*ATL*	*MLB*	*34*	*2*	*2*	*0*	*33*	*0*	*35*	*35*	*6*	*3.6*	*8.7*	*34*	*43%*	*.301*

Comparables: Brandon Lyon, Jeanmar Gómez, Tommy Hunter

At the three-and-a-half-week mark of the 2019 season, Swarzak had come out of the gate firing on all cylinders and making six consecutive scoreless appearances in a row for the Mariners—who added the righty as a cash balancer in the trade that sent Edwin Díaz and Robinson Canó to New York. He then had seven appearances in a row in which he allowed at least one run, and found himself pushed out of Seattle befor Memorial Day.

At the three-and-a-half month mark of the 2019 season, Swarzak was fully on the path to redemption and pitching high-leverage innings for a playoff team. He leaned heavily on his slider and held opposing hitters to a .129/.200/.214 line in his first two months in Atlanta, bringing his seasonal ERA down to 2.31. He then saw a drop in velocity down the stretch and gave up nearly a run an inning until his season ended by being unceremoniously left off the NLDS roster.

At the three-and-a-half decade mark in his time on Earth, Swarzak is inconsistent, unreliable and has gotten the last big payday of his career. That 2017 miracle of a season is a relic of a shoulder that cannot find the strike zone consistently enough to function as anything more than bullpen depth.

YEAR	TEAM	LVL	AGE	WHIP	ERA	DRA	WARP	MPH	FB%	WHF	CSP
2017	CHA	MLB	31	1.03	2.23	2.92	1.2	96.1	48.8	15.5	47.3
2017	MIL	MLB	31	1.03	2.48	3.37	0.6	96.6	48.2	15.3	46.8
2018	NYN	MLB	32	1.59	6.15	5.71	-0.2	96.3	53.5	9.8	46.9
2019	ATL	MLB	33	1.44	4.31	5.48	-0.1	94.9	39.8	12.2	39.9
2019	SEA	MLB	33	1.61	5.27	5.45	0.0	95.6	42.9	13.1	43.7
2020	*ATL*	*MLB*	*34*	*1.41*	*4.66*	*4.86*	*0.2*	*94.6*	*45.2*	*12.8*	*43.8*

Anthony Swarzak, continued

Pitch Shape vs LHH

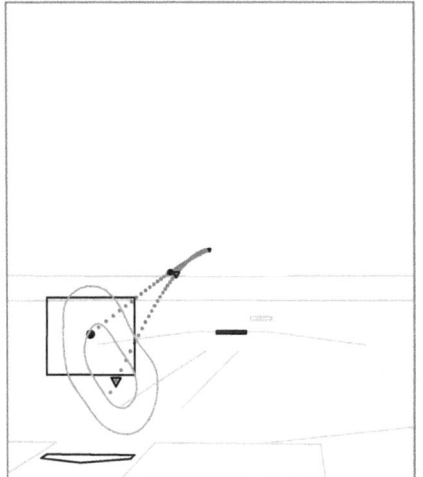

Pitch Shape vs RHH

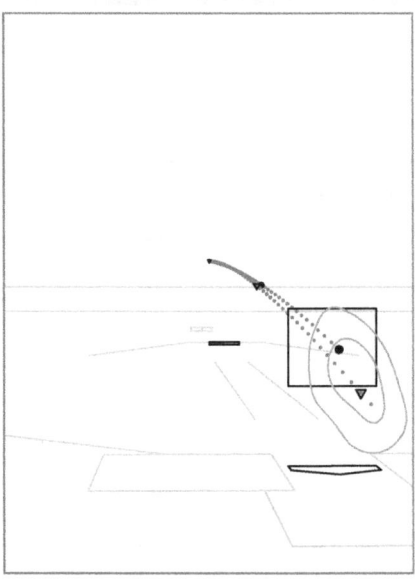

Type	Frequency	Velocity	H Movement	V Movement
● Fastball	37.3%	93.7 [104]	-7.2 [98]	-12.9 [108]
☐ Sinker	3.3%	92.2 [98]	-12.6 [100]	-17.1 [112]
+ Cutter				
▲ Changeup				
✕ Splitter				
▽ Slider	59.4%	86.4 [108]	4.2 [96]	-29.6 [110]
◇ Curveball				
✦ Slow Curveball				
✱ Knuckleball				
▼ Screwball				

Jason Vargas LHP

Born: 02/02/83   Age: 37   Bats: L   Throws: L
Height: 6'0"   Weight: 215   Origin: Round 2, 2004 Draft (#68 overall)

YEAR	TEAM	LVL	AGE	W	L	SV	G	GS	IP	H	HR	BB/9	K/9	K	GB%	BABIP
2017	KCA	MLB	34	18	11	0	32	32	179²	181	27	2.9	6.7	134	41%	.289
2018	BRO	A-	35	0	0	0	2	2	12	7	2	0.0	14.2	19	30%	.238
2018	NYN	MLB	35	7	9	0	20	20	92	100	18	2.9	8.2	84	42%	.307
2019	NYN	MLB	36	6	5	0	19	18	94¹	81	14	3.7	7.7	81	40%	.253
2019	PHI	MLB	36	1	4	0	11	11	55¹	60	7	3.9	7.0	43	40%	.312
2020	PHI	MLB	37	2	2	0	33	0	35	35	7	3.1	7.3	28	39%	.276

Comparables: Bob Ojeda, Bruce Hurst, Frank Viola

Ignore the DRA and WARP that barely made a proverbial dent between the lines. Vargas had an amazing season, a journey that transcended statistics and, in many ways, not only baseball but life itself. Vargas' season was as inspirational as the fictitious *Rochelle, Rochelle's* erotic journey from Milan to Minsk. He scuffled with a New York beat reporter in the Mets clubhouse, was an associate professor at the City University of New York when he wasn't on the mound and was visited by a time traveler from the future during a postgame press conference. In between all these things that may have happened but may have also just been a series of ridiculous memes, Vargas pitched a complete-game shutout and somehow did more for the Mets by sabotaging the Phillies behind enemy lines than he did while he was still in Queens. It isn't easy to make your mark when your stat line is this bad but Vargas somehow managed to capture our hearts and minds, transcend the game and trip the light fantastic by the mere fact of his very existence.

YEAR	TEAM	LVL	AGE	WHIP	ERA	DRA	WARP	MPH	FB%	WHF	CSP
2017	KCA	MLB	34	1.33	4.16	4.48	2.2	87.9	46.8	10.2	45
2018	BRO	A-	35	0.58	1.50	1.72	0.5				
2018	NYN	MLB	35	1.41	5.77	4.11	1.3	88.7	54.4	11.7	47.3
2019	NYN	MLB	36	1.27	4.01	4.73	1.1	87.1	51.4	10.4	44.7
2019	PHI	MLB	36	1.52	5.37	6.15	-0.2	85.8	46.8	10.5	40.2
2020	PHI	MLB	37	1.36	4.88	4.98	0.2	86.2	48.6	10.4	43.8

Philadelphia Phillies 2020

Jason Vargas, continued

Pitch Shape vs LHH

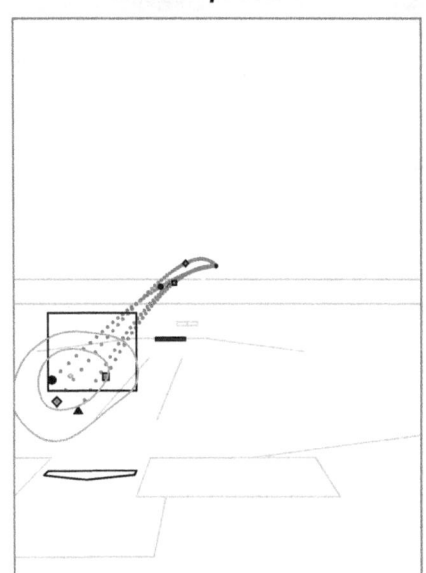

Pitch Shape vs RHH

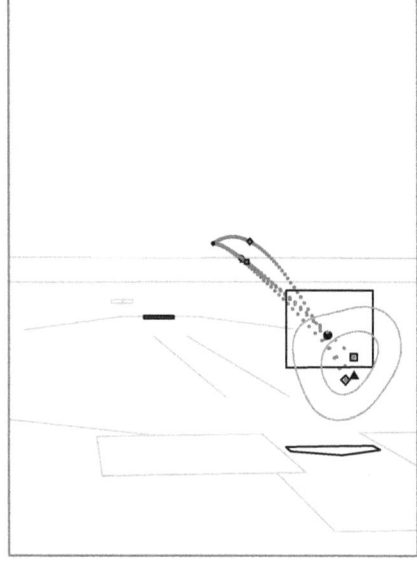

Vince Velasquez RHP

Born: 06/07/92 Age: 28 Bats: R Throws: R
Height: 6'3" Weight: 205 Origin: Round 2, 2010 Draft (#58 overall)

YEAR	TEAM	LVL	AGE	W	L	SV	G	GS	IP	H	HR	BB/9	K/9	K	GB%	BABIP
2017	PHI	MLB	25	2	7	0	15	15	72	74	15	4.2	8.5	68	45%	.303
2018	PHI	MLB	26	9	12	0	31	30	146²	138	16	3.6	9.9	161	41%	.316
2019	PHI	MLB	27	7	8	0	33	23	117¹	120	26	3.3	10.0	130	36%	.305
2020	PHI	MLB	28	8	8	0	51	19	134	128	24	3.7	9.9	148	37%	.298

Comparables: Jon Gray, Luis Castillo, Bud Norris

It didn't happen until four seasons into his Phillies tenure, but the buzz and hope that once surrounded Velasquez has disappeared. Part of this is because 2019 didn't feature the sort of ace-level start Velasquez has delivered in the past that could make fans dream on him once again. Mostly, it is because it was his age-27 season and he has logged over 500 major-league innings with little if any tangible improvement. Velasquez is what he is. He still throws hard, but his secondary stuff has never played up and he still makes way too many mistakes in the meaty part of the zone. Velasquez abandoned his change and relied much more on a slider as his second pitch, which did him no favors. The raw ability and stuff could lead to a dominant season but given the track record if it happens it's more likely to be an anomaly than a breakout.

YEAR	TEAM	LVL	AGE	WHIP	ERA	DRA	WARP	MPH	FB%	WHF	CSP
2017	PHI	MLB	25	1.50	5.12	5.66	-0.1	96.5	68.5	10.1	51.7
2018	PHI	MLB	26	1.34	4.85	4.20	1.9	96.6	64	12.5	50.3
2019	PHI	MLB	27	1.39	4.91	5.46	0.4	96.6	66.7	12.7	46.8
2020	PHI	MLB	28	1.36	4.66	4.63	1.6	96.0	66.3	12.3	49.5

Philadelphia Phillies 2020

Vince Velasquez, continued

Pitch Shape vs LHH

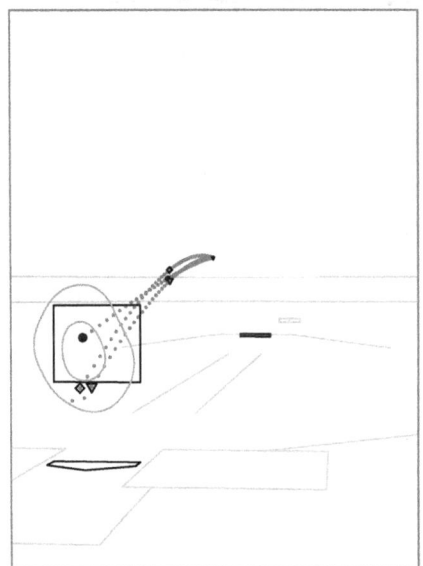

Pitch Shape vs RHH

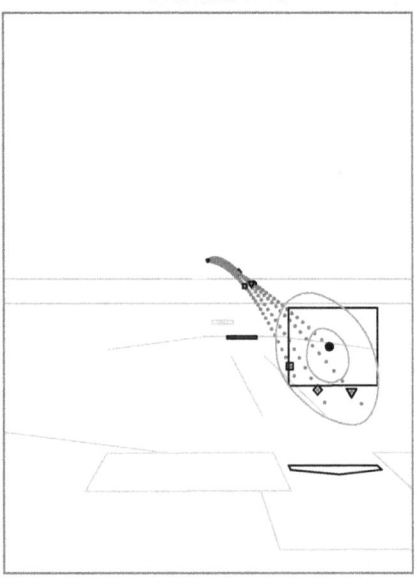

Type	Frequency	Velocity	H Movement	V Movement
● Fastball	62.4%	94.6 [106]	-3.2 [116]	-12.3 [110]
□ Sinker	4.3%	92.9 [102]	-11 [111]	-20.6 [99]
+ Cutter				
▲ Changeup				
✕ Splitter				
▽ Slider	19.8%	86.8 [110]	5.5 [102]	-30.7 [107]
◇ Curveball	12.4%	83.4 [116]	4.6 [88]	-44.1 [107]
⊕ Slow Curveball				
✱ Knuckleball				
▼ Screwball				

Zack Wheeler RHP

Born: 05/30/90   Age: 30   Bats: L   Throws: R
Height: 6'4"   Weight: 195   Origin: Round 1, 2009 Draft (#6 overall)

YEAR	TEAM	LVL	AGE	W	L	SV	G	GS	IP	H	HR	BB/9	K/9	K	GB%	BABIP
2017	NYN	MLB	27	3	7	0	17	17	86^1	97	15	4.2	8.4	81	48%	.332
2018	NYN	MLB	28	12	7	0	29	29	182^1	150	14	2.7	8.8	179	46%	.279
2019	NYN	MLB	29	11	8	0	31	31	195^1	196	22	2.3	9.0	195	45%	.312
2020	PHI	MLB	30	10	9	0	28	28	157	152	20	3.0	9.1	159	45%	.306

Comparables: Alex Cobb, Max Scherzer, Chris Archer

Wheeler and Carlos Gómez were teammates for a brief time after they were famously almost traded for each other in 2015, but it seemed that this was finally going to be the year that Wheeler would be on the move. The team shocked everyone and bought at the deadline instead of selling which meant that the righty finished the year in the orange and blue. Just like his rotation-mates, he featured elite velocity in his repertoire and had another encouragingly healthy season tossing a career-high number of innings. A strong showing in his walk year certainly did his wallet a bunch of good, as the Phillies inked the former sixth-overall pick to a five-year contract worth $118 million and are penciling him in as their second starter behind ace Aaron Nola. He earned it too, as Wheeler's 9.0 WARP over the last two seasons puts him in the top 10 of the National League.

YEAR	TEAM	LVL	AGE	WHIP	ERA	DRA	WARP	MPH	FB%	WHF	CSP
2017	NYN	MLB	27	1.59	5.21	5.30	0.3	97.1	61.7	10	49.5
2018	NYN	MLB	28	1.12	3.31	3.01	4.8	98.7	58.3	12	48.2
2019	NYN	MLB	29	1.26	3.96	3.80	4.2	98.9	59.1	11.6	50.6
2020	PHI	MLB	30	1.31	3.97	4.02	3.1	97.8	59	11.5	49.4

Zack Wheeler, continued

Pitch Shape vs LHH

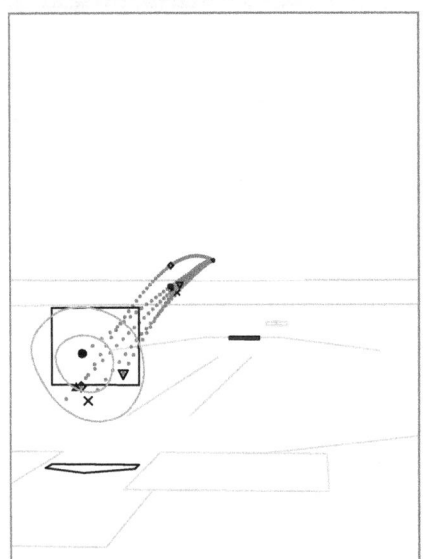

Pitch Shape vs RHH

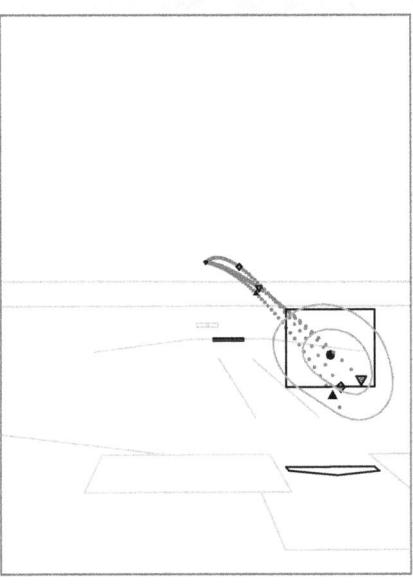

Type	Frequency	Velocity	H Movement	V Movement
● Fastball	59.0%	97 [113]	-10.7 [83]	-13.2 [107]
☐ Sinker				
+ Cutter				
▲ Changeup	9.1%	89.2 [114]	-10.9 [101]	-21.8 [116]
✕ Splitter				
▽ Slider	20.0%	91.5 [130]	2.2 [88]	-23.4 [128]
◇ Curveball	9.9%	80.9 [108]	7.6 [101]	-47.6 [100]
✥ Slow Curveball				
✱ Knuckleball				
▼ Screwball				

José Álvarez LHP

Born: 05/06/89 Age: 31 Bats: L Throws: L
Height: 5'11" Weight: 180 Origin: International Free Agent, 2005

YEAR	TEAM	LVL	AGE	W	L	SV	G	GS	IP	H	HR	BB/9	K/9	K	GB%	BABIP
2017	SLC	AAA	28	0	0	0	9	0	11²	10	0	1.5	7.7	10	44%	.294
2017	LAA	MLB	28	0	3	1	64	0	48²	50	7	2.2	8.3	45	39%	.309
2018	LAA	MLB	29	6	4	1	76	0	63	51	3	3.1	8.4	59	48%	.274
2019	PHI	MLB	30	3	4	1	67	1	59	66	8	2.7	7.8	51	50%	.328
2020	PHI	MLB	31	3	3	0	53	0	56	53	8	2.7	7.9	49	49%	.284

Comparables: Aaron Loup, Bobby Parnell, Rafael Perez

Acquired by the Phillies last winter to bolster their poor numbers against left-handed batters, Álvarez was competent enough as a LOOGY but struggled when asked to face right-handers. This became more of a problem as the season dragged on and Phillies relievers dropped faster than a hapless extra on The Walking Dead. The move from pitcher-friendly Angel Stadium to hitter-friendly Citizens Bank Park didn't do Álvarez any favors either, as his home run rate spiked despite an increase in grounders. It wasn't his fault, but Phillies relievers repeated as the fourth worst group in the majors in 2019 against lefties. Álvarez was fine, but there's only so much a complementary bullpen piece can do when the rest of the bullpen goes full zombie apocalypse.

YEAR	TEAM	LVL	AGE	WHIP	ERA	DRA	WARP	MPH	FB%	WHF	CSP
2017	SLC	AAA	28	1.03	2.31	3.52	0.2				
2017	LAA	MLB	28	1.27	3.88	4.35	0.4	93.2	55.9	12	45.6
2018	LAA	MLB	29	1.16	2.71	3.82	0.8	93.9	57	11.5	47.9
2019	PHI	MLB	30	1.42	3.36	4.90	0.3	93.7	52.6	11.8	48
2020	PHI	MLB	31	1.25	3.84	3.96	0.9	92.8	54.5	11.6	47.1

José Álvarez, continued

Pitch Shape vs LHH

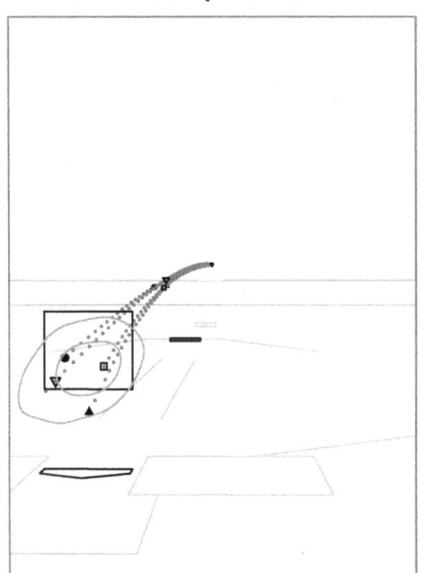

Pitch Shape vs RHH

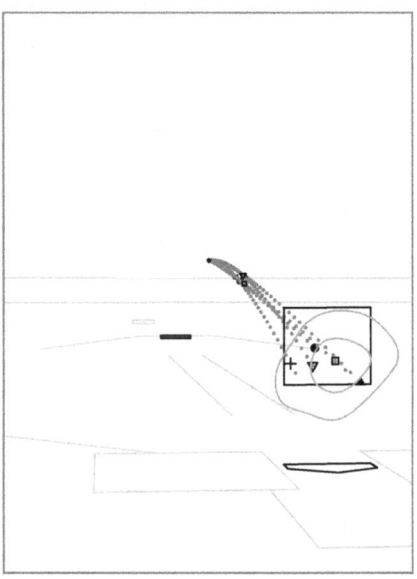

Type	Frequency	Velocity	H Movement	V Movement
● Fastball	15.5%	92 [99]	9.6 [88]	-15.1 [102]
□ Sinker	37.1%	91.7 [96]	15.3 [83]	-19.3 [104]
+ Cutter	5.2%	86.4 [86]	-1.8 [100]	-24.9 [97]
▲ Changeup	21.9%	82.4 [90]	14.2 [86]	-31.9 [87]
× Splitter				
▽ Slider	20.1%	83.6 [97]	-4.1 [96]	-30.9 [106]
◇ Curveball				
⊕ Slow Curveball				
✱ Knuckleball				
▼ Screwball				

PLAYER COMMENTS WITHOUT GRAPHS

Alec Bohm 3B
Born: 08/03/96   Age: 23   Bats: R   Throws: R
Height: 6'5"   Weight: 225   Origin: Round 1, 2018 Draft (#3 overall)

YEAR	TEAM	LVL	AGE	PA	R	2B	3B	HR	RBI	BB	K	SB	CS	AVG/OBP/SLG
2018	PLL	RK	21	27	8	1	1	0	3	2	0	2	0	.391/.481/.522
2018	WPT	A-	21	121	9	5	1	0	12	10	19	1	0	.224/.314/.290
2019	LWD	A	22	93	13	9	0	3	11	12	14	3	0	.367/.441/.595
2019	CLR	A+	22	177	25	10	3	4	27	17	21	1	2	.329/.395/.506
2019	REA	AA	22	270	38	11	1	14	42	28	38	2	2	.269/.344/.500
2020	PHI	MLB	23	280	31	13	1	10	35	21	54	1	0	.256/.317/.433

Comparables: Matt Antonelli, Carlos Asuaje, Adam Duvall

Bohm's prospect status entering 2019 was based far more on projection than performance. The third-overall pick in the 2018 draft missed a month with a knee injury, didn't play in a full-season league and couldn't even clear the fences once in his first taste of pro ball. Yet, he put those concerns to rest with a strong season across three levels, looking like the hitter everyone thought the Phillies drafted: a future stud with the rare combination of plus power and contact. Bohm's glove is another story. He has worked hard on improving his defense, but his slow footwork and lack of instincts at the hot corner are evident. He's going to be an offensive mainstay in Philadelphia regardless of where he plays, but Rhys Hoskins v2.0 at a corner outfield slot or the hot corner isn't optimal for an organization that has struggled to put quality defenders on the diamond of late.

YEAR	TEAM	LVL	AGE	PA	DRC+	VORP	BABIP	BRR	FRAA	WARP
2018	PLL	RK	21	27	147	2.1	.391	-1.6	3B(5): 1.3	0.2
2018	WPT	A-	21	121	89	-0.4	.273	-0.9	3B(20): -2.7	-0.2
2019	LWD	A	22	93	213	14.3	.406	-0.8	3B(14): -0.8, 1B(5): -0.1	1.1
2019	CLR	A+	22	177	173	18.1	.358	0.8	3B(25): 1.1, 1B(7): 0.6	2.0
2019	REA	AA	22	270	154	16.4	.265	-0.7	3B(43): 0.0, 1B(12): -0.8	2.1
2020	PHI	MLB	23	280	96	4.9	.290	-0.4	3B -1	0.5

Luis Garcia MI

Born: 10/01/00 Age: 19 Bats: B Throws: R
Height: 5'11" Weight: 170 Origin: International Free Agent, 2017

YEAR	TEAM	LVL	AGE	PA	R	2B	3B	HR	RBI	BB	K	SB	CS	AVG/OBP/SLG
2018	PLL	RK	17	187	33	11	3	1	32	15	21	12	8	.369/.433/.488
2019	LWD	A	18	524	36	14	3	4	36	44	132	9	8	.186/.261/.255
2020	PHI	MLB	19	251	20	11	1	3	21	18	71	4	2	.208/.271/.304

Comparables: Jefry Marte, Carson Kelly, Cheslor Cuthbert

Garcia struggled mightily in his first taste of full-season ball. He looked overmatched most of the year, his diminutive size serving to his disadvantage as even when Garcia made contact, he had difficulty making it count. All this means little if anything in terms of Garcia's long-term outlook. He has solid barrel control and bat speed, is still a good-looking defender up the middle and is eventually going to grow into that gangly frame of his. He was also one of only four 18-year-old players who logged significant time in the Sally League. All Garcia's poor 2019 means is that he is on a longer developmental path; he has plenty of time to break out and live up to the hype that made him such a prized signing in 2017.

YEAR	TEAM	LVL	AGE	PA	DRC+	VORP	BABIP	BRR	FRAA	WARP
2018	PLL	RK	17	187	196	22.6	.418	-0.1	SS(43): -2.1	2.2
2019	LWD	A	18	524	58	-9.8	.247	-5.0	SS(71): -0.2, 2B(55): -5.3	-1.4
2020	PHI	MLB	19	251	55	-6.8	.284	-0.3	SS -1, 2B -1	-0.9

Mickey Moniak CF

Born: 05/13/98 Age: 22 Bats: L Throws: R
Height: 6'2" Weight: 185 Origin: Round 1, 2016 Draft (#1 overall)

YEAR	TEAM	LVL	AGE	PA	R	2B	3B	HR	RBI	BB	K	SB	CS	AVG/OBP/SLG
2017	LWD	A	19	509	53	22	6	5	44	28	109	11	7	.236/.284/.341
2018	CLR	A+	20	465	50	28	3	5	55	22	100	6	5	.270/.304/.383
2019	REA	AA	21	504	63	28	13	11	67	33	111	15	3	.252/.303/.439
2020	PHI	MLB	22	251	21	13	2	5	25	14	68	2	1	.221/.269/.358

Comparables: Xavier Avery, Dustin Fowler, Rey Fuentes

If Moniak wasn't a first-overall pick who took home a $6 million signing bonus, he'd be likely be lumped in with all the lineouts at the end of this chapter. He wasn't overmatched or completely out of his element at Double-A Reading but the hitch in his swing, the poor pitch recognition on high spin offerings and his difficulties with same-side hurlers led to another nondescript season. Moniak's most probable path to the majors is as a fourth outfielder, and while he is only 21 there is nothing buried in either his stat line or the intense scouting of the last three and a half years that provide any legitimate hope that he can live up to the expectations that should go along with the 1-1 pick in the draft. For the faceless, nameless version of Moniak, however, a potential everyday role in the outfield would be a realistically achievable success.

YEAR	TEAM	LVL	AGE	PA	DRC+	VORP	BABIP	BRR	FRAA	WARP
2017	LWD	A	19	509	84	12.6	.292	-0.1	CF(115): -9.8	-0.3
2018	CLR	A+	20	465	84	6.5	.334	-0.1	CF(99): -7.3, LF(9): -0.3	-0.1
2019	REA	AA	21	504	97	20.9	.307	1.4	CF(93): -2.2, RF(24): 0.5	1.3
2020	PHI	MLB	22	251	63	-4.0	.289	0.0	CF -2, RF 0	-0.7

Bryson Stott SS

Born: 10/06/97   Age: 22   Bats: L   Throws: R
Height: 6'3"   Weight: 200   Origin: Round 1, 2019 Draft (#14 overall)

YEAR	TEAM	LVL	AGE	PA	R	2B	3B	HR	RBI	BB	K	SB	CS	AVG/OBP/SLG
2019	WPT	A-	21	182	27	8	2	5	24	22	39	5	3	.274/.370/.446
2020	PHI	MLB	22	251	24	12	1	7	27	16	71	2	1	.226/.282/.376

Comparables: Tyler Greene, Brent Lillibridge, J.D. Davis

For the third consecutive year, the Phillies took a college hitter in the first round, selecting the UNLV product in the first round and quickly inking him to a $3.9 million signing bonus. Stott's polished, all-around game translated well to his professional debut, and he was one of the best hitters in the New York-Penn League right out of the gate. Stott isn't a high-end, tools-first prospect, but has the chance to excel because of his strong work ethic and a lack of any significant holes in his game. He has drawn comparison to Giants shortstop Brandon Crawford, and Stott - an avid viewer of baseball clips on YouTube - agrees it's a pretty accurate assessment. Stott should move quickly, giving the Phillies a Bryce/Bryson Las Vegas tandem for years to come.

YEAR	TEAM	LVL	AGE	PA	DRC+	VORP	BABIP	BRR	FRAA	WARP
2019	WPT	A-	21	182	149	17.7	.336	1.1	SS(33): -1.0, 2B(2): -0.1	1.4
2020	PHI	MLB	22	251	74	-0.3	.295	0.0	SS 0, 2B 0	0.0

Enyel De Los Santos RHP
Born: 12/25/95 Age: 24 Bats: R Throws: R
Height: 6'3" Weight: 170 Origin: International Free Agent, 2014

YEAR	TEAM	LVL	AGE	W	L	SV	G	GS	IP	H	HR	BB/9	K/9	K	GB%	BABIP
2017	SAN	AA	21	10	6	0	26	24	150	131	12	2.9	8.3	138	45%	.290
2018	LEH	AAA	22	10	5	0	22	22	126²	104	12	3.1	7.8	110	42%	.264
2018	PHI	MLB	22	1	0	0	7	2	19	19	2	3.8	7.1	15	51%	.309
2019	LEH	AAA	23	5	7	0	19	19	94	81	16	3.4	7.9	83	39%	.256
2019	PHI	MLB	23	0	1	0	5	1	11	13	4	4.1	7.4	9	41%	.321
2020	PHI	MLB	24	3	4	0	24	8	57	57	10	3.1	7.6	48	40%	.286

Comparables: Jake Odorizzi, Brandon Maurer, Reynaldo López

It was telling that despite the Phillies' various needs in both their rotation and bullpen throughout the season that De Los Santos couldn't crack either and spent most of the year in the minors as an emergency option. The Dominican native has the same problem most pitchers who get stuck with the Quad-A label do. He has a strong, low-90s sinking fastball and a major-league-ready change but his neither of his breakers are anything special and there isn't enough separation between his slider and curve. De Los Santos' odds of making it as a back-end starter continue to diminish, and he looks more and more like a future bullpen piece.

YEAR	TEAM	LVL	AGE	WHIP	ERA	DRA	WARP	MPH	FB%	WHF	CSP
2017	SAN	AA	21	1.19	3.78	4.21	1.7				
2018	LEH	AAA	22	1.16	2.63	3.60	2.8				
2018	PHI	MLB	22	1.42	4.74	4.97	0.0	97.4	60.3	10.8	50.2
2019	LEH	AAA	23	1.23	4.40	3.99	2.5				
2019	PHI	MLB	23	1.64	7.36	4.75	0.1	96.3	59.1	12.5	53.5
2020	PHI	MLB	24	1.34	4.68	4.74	0.6	96.7	61.6	11.8	53.6

Spencer Howard RHP

Born: 07/28/96 Age: 23 Bats: R Throws: R
Height: 6'2" Weight: 205 Origin: Round 2, 2017 Draft (#45 overall)

YEAR	TEAM	LVL	AGE	W	L	SV	G	GS	IP	H	HR	BB/9	K/9	K	GB%	BABIP
2017	WPT	A-	20	1	1	0	9	9	28^1	22	0	5.7	12.7	40	48%	.349
2018	LWD	A	21	9	8	0	23	23	112	101	6	3.2	11.8	147	40%	.349
2019	CLR	A+	22	2	1	0	7	7	35	19	1	1.3	12.3	48	44%	.261
2019	REA	AA	22	1	0	0	6	6	30^2	20	2	2.6	11.2	38	42%	.242
2020	PHI	MLB	23	2	2	0	33	0	35	34	5	3.3	10.8	42	41%	.327

Comparables: Dylan Cease, Hunter Wood, José De León

Initially, the buzz surrounding Howard was muted after he missed the first two months of the season with shoulder pain. Not only did the top prospect not miss a beat when he returned from injury, but he elevated his game down the stretch, tightening his command and improving his already solid secondary offerings even further. Howard's filthy three-pitch arsenal includes a mid-90s fastball he can dial up to 7s and 8s, a splitter-esque plus change that's difficult for opposing hitters to pick up and a slider with some of the nastiest, late-breaking bite you're going to see in the minors. Howard is on the fast track to the majors. Regardless of whether he arrives on Opening Day or later in the year, he's going to have one of the more electrifying debuts of 2020 if his health permits.

YEAR	TEAM	LVL	AGE	WHIP	ERA	DRA	WARP	MPH	FB%	WHF	CSP
2017	WPT	A-	20	1.41	4.45	4.13	0.4				
2018	LWD	A	21	1.26	3.78	3.87	1.8				
2019	CLR	A+	22	0.69	1.29	2.25	1.2				
2019	REA	AA	22	0.95	2.35	2.93	0.8				
2020	PHI	MLB	23	1.35	4.33	4.45	0.4				

Damon Jones   LHP
Born: 09/30/94   Age: 25   Bats: L   Throws: L
Height: 6'5"   Weight: 225   Origin: Round 18, 2017 Draft (#533 overall)

YEAR	TEAM	LVL	AGE	W	L	SV	G	GS	IP	H	HR	BB/9	K/9	K	GB%	BABIP
2017	WPT	A-	22	2	3	3	13	0	26	23	0	6.9	13.2	38	52%	.377
2018	LWD	A	23	10	7	0	23	22	113¹	105	7	4.0	9.8	123	58%	.326
2019	CLR	A+	24	4	3	0	11	11	58¹	38	3	3.7	13.6	88	61%	.310
2019	REA	AA	24	1	0	0	4	4	22	9	0	3.7	12.7	31	52%	.225
2019	LEH	AAA	24	0	1	0	8	8	34	27	4	6.9	8.7	33	52%	.258
2020	*PHI*	*MLB*	*25*	*2*	*2*	*0*	*33*	*0*	*35*	*34*	*5*	*3.9*	*10.6*	*41*	*46%*	*.321*

Comparables: Anthony Kay, Wei-Chieh Huang, Rico Garcia

A 18th round pick in the 2017 draft, Jones was a senior sign with nothing more than a hard fastball, poor control and no polish. The Phillies developmental team got their hands on him, and the combination of organizational patience and Jones' hard work unlocked a 91-94 mph heater with good movement, a solid changeup and a slurvy breaking ball that's eminently usable. The usual caveats about an older hurler dominating younger competition in the Florida State League apply but tall, hard throwing southpaws don't grow on trees. Jones has elevated himself significantly in the Philadelphia prospect pantheon and has put himself in the conversation for a potential major league debut in 2020.

YEAR	TEAM	LVL	AGE	WHIP	ERA	DRA	WARP	MPH	FB%	WHF	CSP
2017	WPT	A-	22	1.65	4.85	5.67	-0.2				
2018	LWD	A	23	1.37	3.41	4.82	0.5				
2019	CLR	A+	24	1.06	1.54	3.12	1.4				
2019	REA	AA	24	0.82	0.82	2.63	0.6				
2019	LEH	AAA	24	1.56	6.62	5.03	0.6				
2020	*PHI*	*MLB*	*25*	*1.42*	*4.70*	*4.64*	*0.3*				

Adonis Medina   RHP

Born: 12/18/96   Age: 23   Bats: R   Throws: R
Height: 6'1"   Weight: 185   Origin: International Free Agent, 2014

YEAR	TEAM	LVL	AGE	W	L	SV	G	GS	IP	H	HR	BB/9	K/9	K	GB%	BABIP
2017	LWD	A	20	4	9	0	22	22	119²	103	7	2.9	10.0	133	49%	.306
2018	CLR	A+	21	10	4	0	22	21	111¹	103	11	2.9	9.9	123	51%	.316
2019	REA	AA	22	7	7	0	22	21	105²	103	11	3.5	7.0	82	47%	.287
2020	PHI	MLB	23	1	2	0	5	5	24	25	4	3.9	6.4	17	44%	.278

Comparables: Yennsy Diaz, Miguel Almonte, Paul Blackburn

It was more of the same in 2019 for Medina, a prospect whose stuff is tantalizingly great at its best and frustratingly inconsistent at its worst. When he's on, Medina hits 96-97 on the gun, throws a plus breaker, flashes an average change and looks like a future mid-tier starting pitcher. When he isn't the velocity disappears, the secondary pitches lack bite and consistency and his endurance is questionable. Reading is a tough place to pitch, and Medina's home ERA (6.14) was much worse than on the road (3.92) but his struggles weren't solely related to the venue. There was some talk of promoting Medina in September to help the big club's depleted pen, but the team decided rest was the better long-term option. A future as a multi-inning, Seranthony Domínguez type reliever is possible, but for now the Phillies are committed to seeing if Medina can make it as a starter.

YEAR	TEAM	LVL	AGE	WHIP	ERA	DRA	WARP	MPH	FB%	WHF	CSP
2017	LWD	A	20	1.19	3.01	4.29	1.4				
2018	CLR	A+	21	1.25	4.12	4.73	0.8				
2019	REA	AA	22	1.36	4.94	5.99	-1.3				
2020	PHI	MLB	23	1.45	5.30	5.22	0.2				

Francisco Morales   RHP

Born: 10/27/99   Age: 20   Bats: R   Throws: R
Height: 6'4"   Weight: 185   Origin: International Free Agent, 2016

YEAR	TEAM	LVL	AGE	W	L	SV	G	GS	IP	H	HR	BB/9	K/9	K	GB%	BABIP
2017	PHL	RK	17	3	2	0	10	9	41^1	34	1	4.4	9.6	44	44%	.308
2018	WPT	A-	18	4	5	0	13	13	56^1	54	6	5.3	10.9	68	42%	.324
2019	LWD	A	19	1	8	1	27	15	96^2	82	8	4.3	12.0	129	46%	.325
2020	PHI	MLB	20	2	2	0	33	0	35	36	6	4.0	9.4	37	40%	.313

Comparables: JC Ramírez, Joel Payamps, Fabio Castillo

A teenage arm with a ton of talent and a lack of polish, Morales' large frame gives him the all-too-common combination of power and trouble repeating his delivery—which leads to a poor command profile. His fastball is an overpowering pitch that can get to the upper 90s on the gun and Morales has a slider he can throw at varying velocities and spin rates, but he lacks a quality third pitch. While his size and strength can easily overpower most hitters in the low minors, his inconsistency and inability to pitch in or near the zone will expose him against more advanced hitters. He'll only be 20 on Opening Day so there is plenty of time for things to click, but for these types of pitchers, turbulence is to be expected.

YEAR	TEAM	LVL	AGE	WHIP	ERA	DRA	WARP	MPH	FB%	WHF	CSP
2017	PHL	RK	17	1.31	3.05	5.16	0.4				
2018	WPT	A-	18	1.54	5.27	6.11	-0.6				
2019	LWD	A	19	1.32	3.82	4.39	0.7				
2020	PHI	MLB	20	1.47	5.10	5.08	0.1				

JoJo Romero LHP

Born: 09/09/96   Age: 23   Bats: L   Throws: L
Height: 5'11"   Weight: 190   Origin: Round 4, 2016 Draft (#107 overall)

YEAR	TEAM	LVL	AGE	W	L	SV	G	GS	IP	H	HR	BB/9	K/9	K	GB%	BABIP
2017	LWD	A	20	5	1	0	13	13	76^2	61	2	2.5	9.3	79	60%	.299
2017	CLR	A+	20	5	2	0	10	10	52^1	43	2	2.6	8.4	49	52%	.289
2018	REA	AA	21	7	6	0	18	18	106^2	97	13	3.5	8.4	100	53%	.286
2019	REA	AA	22	4	4	0	11	11	57^2	58	4	1.9	8.1	52	50%	.321
2019	LEH	AAA	22	3	5	0	13	13	53^2	68	8	5.9	6.7	40	50%	.345
2020	PHI	MLB	23	3	3	0	10	10	49	48	8	3.7	6.5	35	47%	.274

Comparables: Steve Garrison, Yohander Méndez, Brock Burke

The stat line finally caught up with the cautious scouting reports, and 2019 was a big step back for Romero developmentally. His unorthodox, three-quarters arm action gave hitters difficulty in the low minors but hasn't been nearly as effective as Romero has moved up the ladder. He isn't missing many bats, and while his sinker/change combination does lead to a fair number of grounders it's not enough to stop more advanced batters from teeing off when he misses his spots. Romero could still fit in as a back-end starter, but like a lot of arms in the Phillies system is looking more and more like a future reliever.

YEAR	TEAM	LVL	AGE	WHIP	ERA	DRA	WARP	MPH	FB%	WHF	CSP
2017	LWD	A	20	1.07	2.11	3.77	1.4				
2017	CLR	A+	20	1.11	2.24	4.00	0.8				
2018	REA	AA	21	1.29	3.80	4.23	1.4				
2019	REA	AA	22	1.21	4.84	4.99	0.0				
2019	LEH	AAA	22	1.92	6.88	7.96	-0.6				
2020	PHI	MLB	23	1.39	4.65	4.69	0.6				

LINEOUTS

Hitters

HITTER	POS	TEAM	LVL	AGE	PA	R	2B	3B	HR	RBI	BB	K	SB	CS	AVG/OBP/SLG	DRC+	WARP
Daniel Brito	2B	CLR	A+	21	379	37	14	1	4	32	22	73	6	10	.243/.296/.325	81	2.4
Arquimedes Gamboa	SS	REA	AA	21	421	35	10	5	3	28	59	112	21	8	.188/.305/.270	73	0.6
Phil Gosselin	UT	PHI	MLB	30	68	5	3	0	0	7	3	16	0	0	.262/.294/.308	74	0.0
	UT	LEH	AAA	30	353	54	20	5	8	47	46	61	3	2	.314/.405/.497	136	2.5
Deivy Grullon	C	LEH	AAA	23	457	55	24	0	21	77	45	133	1	0	.283/.354/.496	115	0.9
	C	PHI	MLB	23	9	0	0	1	0	0	1	2	0	0	.111/.111/.222	93	0.0
Nick Hundley	C	LEH	AAA	35	36	2	1	0	1	3	2	17	0	0	.125/.167/.250	16	-0.3
	C	OAK	MLB	35	73	5	3	1	2	5	2	18	0	1	.200/.233/.357	72	-0.3
Andrew Knapp	C	PHI	MLB	27	160	12	9	0	2	8	18	51	0	0	.213/.318/.324	70	0.2
Mikie Mahtook	CF	TOL	AAA	29	415	64	17	1	21	56	51	106	14	7	.260/.357/.492	119	1.6
	CF	DET	MLB	29	25	0	0	0	0	0	2	11	0	0	.000/.080/.000	52	-0.1
Rafael Marchan	C	LWD	A	20	265	21	16	0	0	20	24	31	1	3	.271/.347/.339	130	2.1
	C	CLR	A+	20	86	6	4	0	0	3	6	8	1	2	.231/.291/.282	84	0.2
Nick Maton	MI	CLR	A+	22	384	35	14	3	5	45	41	71	11	8	.276/.358/.380	127	1.6
	MI	REA	AA	22	72	6	3	0	2	6	9	14	1	1	.210/.306/.355	94	0.2
Logan Morrison	1B	PHI	MLB	31	38	5	1	0	2	3	3	10	0	0	.200/.263/.400	89	0.0
	1B	LEH	AAA	31	69	7	5	0	3	12	7	12	0	0	.356/.435/.593	151	1.4
	1B	SWB	AAA	31	164	29	11	0	15	37	8	26	0	1	.289/.341/.658	142	1.4
Simon Muzziotti	CF	CLR	A+	20	465	52	21	3	3	28	32	60	21	12	.287/.337/.372	108	2.2
Jhailyn Ortiz	RF	CLR	A+	20	478	57	15	3	19	65	36	149	2	3	.200/.272/.381	76	1.1
Jose Pirela	OF	PHI	MLB	29	19	1	1	0	1	2	2	4	0	0	.235/.316/.471	78	0.0
	OF	LEH	AAA	29	130	19	9	0	4	14	8	25	2	0	.281/.331/.455	105	0.7
	OF	SDN	MLB	29	5	0	0	0	0	0	0	3	0	0	.000/.000/.000	70	0.0
	OF	ELP	AAA	29	242	50	13	2	18	59	17	51	0	1	.353/.401/.674	126	0.9
T.J. Rivera	INF	HAR	AA	30	41	4	3	0	0	4	3	8	0	0	.237/.293/.316	83	0.0
Sean Rodriguez	INF	LEH	AAA	34	49	7	2	1	4	12	3	19	0	0	.267/.327/.622	84	0.0
	INF	PHI	MLB	34	139	24	5	0	4	12	19	41	1	1	.223/.348/.375	76	0.0
Johan Rojas	OF	PLL	Rk	18	84	13	6	5	0	4	9	12	3	2	.311/.393/.527	147	1.0
	OF	WPT	A-	18	172	17	5	6	2	11	5	29	11	4	.244/.273/.384	82	-0.1
Ronald Torreyes	UT	ROC	AAA	26	330	48	11	1	11	42	12	33	2	1	.256/.289/.406	73	0.3
	UT	MIN	MLB	26	17	3	0	0	0	1	0	3	1	0	.188/.235/.188	83	0.0

Daniel Brito has a pretty swing, but this aesthetic beauty hasn't manifested into raw results since his 2016 campaign in Rookie ball and 2020 will mark the third consecutive make-or-break year for the Phillies' second baseman. Ⓡ **Arquimedes Gamboa** is the real deal defensively but his offense is so bad it doesn't even pass muster in Double-A. Perhaps he's young enough to develop some power, but realistically he profiles as a second-division starting shortstop in 1975. Ⓡ Half of **Phil Gosselin**'s plate appearances in 2019 were as a pinch hitter, a role for which the light-hitting middle infielder seems a wee bit miscast.

⚾ A defensive specialist who has been praised in particular for his elite throwing skills, **Deivy Grullon** profiles as a backup catcher with decent power but too many flaws in his offensive game to make it as a starter. ⚾ The best swindlers know when it's time to go for the lump sum versus when it's better to milk someone dry over the long haul. **Nick Hundley** isn't a con man, but he's finished below replacement level in three of the last four seasons while clearing nearly $9 million. Even after a miserable 2019, which saw him released by the Phillies in August without so much as a big-league appearance, he's probably doing all right at doing all right. ⚾ In an era where most teams are electing to job share and split duties behind the plate, it's a cruel twist of fate that **Andrew Knapp** was buried on the bench behind the most durable and arguably the best catcher in baseball. ⚾ **Mikie Mahtook** became the eighth position player to finish at least 0-for-20 (23) in his fifth major league season or later. We knew Eugenio Velez, and you sir, are no Eugenio Velez. ⚾ One of the Phillies top prospects based mostly on projectability, **Rafael Marchan** made great strides with his defense behind the plate while displaying plus bat speed with a strong line-drive swing that hasn't translated into results just yet. ⚾ The younger brother of big-league reliever Phil, **Nick Maton** is an undersized middle infield prospect who has outperformed his modest scouting projection thus far on both sides of the ball and will get his first extended taste of the high minors this year. ⚾ A beneficiary of the juiced ball in 2017, **Logan Morrison** found himself a victim this time around, as younger and more talented hitters blocked his path to the majors. Morrison spent most of his time punishing Triple-A pitching, at least when he wasn't hurt or being DFA'd. ⚾ Scooped up by the Phillies in 2016 because the Red Sox couldn't follow international free agency rules, **Simon Muzziotti** has proven to be a solid all-around player whose lack of power limits his ceiling to average centerfielder but also squarely puts him at risk of being cast as a spare. ⚾ The Phillies have pushed **Jhailyn Ortiz** aggressively through their system, thus far with poor results. Ortiz's raw power and strong arm are plus-plus tools, but poor contact skills will bestow upon him the dreaded Quad-A label unless there is a significant change in approach. ⚾ Squeezed out of an overcrowded Padres outfield, **Jose Pirela** spent most of the year at Triple-A terrorizing PCL pitching. The Phillies acquired him as minor-league depth and later activated him as a barely used reserve down the stretch. ⚾ **T.J. Rivera** had an unusually tough road back from Tommy John surgery for a hitter, ending up where many former Met flashes in the pan go: the Long Island Ducks. Now back in affiliated ball, he seeks to recapture his form as a hit-first utility man. ⚾ **Sean Rodríguez** logged time at every position for the Phillies except catcher, but for the third year in a row was mostly replacement-level filler whose utility barely outweighed his lack of contributions across the board. ⚾ **Johan Rojas** plays center like his fanny is on fire and has speed and raw power to boot. Alas, the hit tool needs quite a bit of development. ⚾ **Ronald Torreyes** failed to bolster his case as a lucky charm. He logged just seven games down the stretch for an already-good Twins team before getting cast out into the flaming dumpster that is free agency for utility players.

Pitchers

PITCHER	TEAM	LVL	AGE	W	L	SV	G	GS	IP	H	HR	BB/9	K/9	K	GB%	WHIP	ERA	DRA	WARP
Drew Anderson	LEH	AAA	25	0	6	0	11	11	48^1	48	9	5.0	7.4	40	41%	1.55	5.77	4.81	0.9
	PHI	MLB	25	0	0	0	2	0	6	6	1	9.0	9.0	6	44%	2.00	7.50	5.54	0.0
Victor Arano	PHI	MLB	24	1	0	0	3	0	4^2	2	1	3.9	13.5	7	29%	0.86	3.86	4.99	0.0
Garrett Cleavinger	REA	AA	25	3	2	0	34	0	51^2	32	2	5.9	14.5	83	46%	1.28	3.66	3.97	0.4
Austin Davis	LEH	AAA	26	4	1	3	37	0	52^1	43	2	4.1	11.0	64	40%	1.28	2.75	3.29	1.5
	PHI	MLB	26	0	0	0	14	0	20^2	22	6	6.1	10.5	24	40%	1.74	6.53	5.65	-0.1
Edgar Garcia	LEH	AAA	22	2	1	8	25	0	29	15	4	2.5	11.8	38	30%	0.79	2.48	2.01	1.2
	PHI	MLB	22	2	0	0	37	0	39	38	11	6.0	10.4	45	34%	1.64	5.77	5.81	-0.2
J.D. Hammer	REA	AA	24	1	0	2	13	0	20^1	17	1	1.8	11.5	26	51%	1.03	1.77	3.67	0.2
	LEH	AAA	24	2	2	0	17	0	15^2	20	4	8.6	9.2	16	26%	2.23	12.64	8.29	-0.3
	PHI	MLB	24	1	0	0	20	0	19	15	2	5.7	6.2	13	41%	1.42	3.79	6.43	-0.2
Tommy Hunter	PHI	MLB	32	0	0	0	5	0	5^1	2	0	0.0	8.4	5	31%	0.38	0.00	5.14	0.0
Cole Irvin	LEH	AAA	25	6	1	0	17	16	93^2	113	13	1.3	6.2	65	42%	1.36	3.94	4.54	1.9
	PHI	MLB	25	2	1	1	16	3	41^2	45	7	2.8	6.7	31	34%	1.39	5.83	6.80	-0.6
Trevor Kelley	PAW	AAA	25	5	5	12	52	0	65^1	51	8	2.9	8.7	63	34%	1.10	1.79	3.13	2.0
	BOS	MLB	25	0	3	0	10	0	8^1	9	2	5.4	6.5	6	17%	1.68	8.64	7.05	-0.2
Mauricio Llovera	REA	AA	23	3	4	0	14	12	65^1	60	7	3.9	9.9	72	43%	1.35	4.55	4.70	0.2
Erik Miller	WPT	A-	21	0	0	0	6	4	20	13	0	3.2	13.1	29	54%	1.00	0.90	2.34	0.6
	LWD	A	21	1	0	0	3	2	13	10	0	4.2	11.8	17	32%	1.23	2.08	4.31	0.1
Pat Neshek	PHI	MLB	38	0	1	3	20	0	18	23	5	1.0	4.5	9	41%	1.39	5.00	6.40	-0.2
Cristopher Sanchez	BGR	A	22	3	1	2	11	4	40^1	28	3	2.5	8.3	37	56%	0.97	2.01	3.02	0.9
	PCH	A+	22	1	0	0	12	6	34	28	0	3.4	9.5	36	55%	1.21	1.85	4.68	0.1
Robert Stock	ELP	AAA	29	3	0	0	25	3	28^1	36	6	6.0	12.7	40	54%	1.94	4.13	5.58	0.2
	SDN	MLB	29	1	0	0	10	0	10^2	14	2	6.8	12.7	15	50%	2.06	10.12	3.86	0.2
Dan Straily	LEH	AAA	30	1	4	0	6	6	33	33	5	2.5	8.2	30	47%	1.27	5.18	4.38	0.7
	NOR	AAA	30	4	0	0	6	6	34	24	4	2.1	10.1	38	41%	0.94	2.38	4.69	0.7
	BAL	MLB	30	2	4	0	14	8	47^2	73	22	4.2	6.2	33	27%	1.99	9.82		

A once promising prospect for the Phillies, **Drew Anderson**'s command and velocity disappeared, and he was unceremoniously released by the organization in early September. ⓧ Considered by some scouts to possess the best bullpen arm in the organization, **Vìctor Arano** had a bone spur removed from his elbow in May and missed nearly the entire season. ⓧ There are only so many jobs available in which having 'cleaving' in your name actually feels appropriate. Since Viking warrior is off the table as a career path, **Garrett Cleavinger** has turned to mowing down opposing hitters, an art he appeared to master at Double-A in 2019. ⓧ **Austin Davis** rode the Pennsylvania Turnpike Extension shuttle between Philadelphia and Lehigh Valley 14 times in 2019, making him the area's foremost expert on the pointless and neverending competition between local convenience store chains Wawa and Sheetz (they sell gasoline and sandwiches!). ⓫ An inconsistent two-pitch reliever, **Edgar Garcia** struggled in his major league debut as he suffered through an utter lack of command and was so inviting to left-handed batters that by September they were bring bottles of wine up to the plate. ⓫ MC Hammer was a rapper who rose to fame in 1990 for his rap single "U Can't Touch This." **J.D. Hammer** is a reliever for the Philadelphia Phillies. MC's signature look involved a pair of baggy pants. J.D.'s signature look is tied to his distinctive, dark-framed glasses. Hammer's stuff is good, but hitters can most definitely touch it. ⓫ **Tommy Hunter** was at the front of the injury parade of Phillies relievers, marching past the Liberty Bell and Independence Hall, up Benjamin Franklin Parkway to the Philadelphia Art Museum and Eastern State Penitentiary, ultimately disappearing into the bowels of The Mutter Museum to scavenge for new bones and sinews, as both team and city tradition demand of their fallen. ⓫ **Cole Irvin** was overmatched and hit hard in his major-league debut, although he quietly put up a strong September for the Phillies in a middle relief role, which might be where his future lies. ⓫ Generic low-leverage reliever **Trevor Kelley** continued his slow and steady ascent through the organization, earning his first cup of coffee in July. He was lit up by major leaguers in his limited exposure, proving that not every right-handed Kelley has Great Stuff™ ⓫ **Mauricio Llovera** possesses a three-pitch mix that could make him a future back-end starter, but his stuff plays up in the bullpen. He hails from El Tigre, Venezuela, which our dogeared Spanish/English dictionary informs us loosely translates to "The Tiger, Venezuela." ⓫ One of the most talented pitchers in the 2019 draft, **Erik Miller** slipped to the fourth round due to concerns about inconsistency and lack of command. The Phillies hope their track record with similar college pitchers gives them a future mid-tier starter. ⓫ Unless you're Doctor Who, time catches up to us all. **Pat Neshek** is not one of the 13 incarnations of the Gallifreyan Time Lord and found his offerings getting exterminated far too often by opposing batters in between stints on the IL that seemed to last an eternity. ⓫ The Phillies picked up promising pop-up arm **Cristopher Sanchez** from the Rays just before Rule 5 protects were due. He pitched well at both A-ball levels in 2019 and has mid-rotation potential as a three-pitch lefty. ⓫ After getting washed off the Padres roster by their incoming tide of high-octane arms, **Robert Stock** will try out his Three True Outcomes pitching act in Philadelphia this year. ⓫ The Orioles acquired **Dan Straily** to eat innings and save wear and tear on the team's young arms, but the cost of that many baseballs was just too much, even for the rebuilding Birds. Philadelphia acquired Straily in July, this time to devour those innings in Triple-A.

Phillies Prospects

The State of the System

The Phillies farm system has steadily diminished as they transition to win-now mode, but they may have a few more cards to play in 2020.

The Top Ten

1 ★ ★ ★ *2020 Top 101 Prospect* **#36** ★ ★ ★

Spencer Howard   RHP   OFP: 60   ETA: 2020
Born: 07/28/96   Age: 23   Bats: R   Throws: R   Height: 6'2"   Weight: 205
Origin: Round 2, 2017 Draft (#45 overall)

The Report: Spencer Howard had a breakout at the end of the 2018 season, leading to anticipation about how quickly he could move through the organization during the 2019 season. The Phillies conservatively did not double-jump him past Clearwater. Instead, an early season arm injury cost him two months and delayed his promotion to Double-A until late July. In addition to the missed time, it meant that it was over four months into the season until the late 2018 version of Howard took the mound.

Once he did get fully healthy to end the season Howard was back to sitting mid 90s, touching 99. Howard did lose velocity during his starts, but that could potentially be attributed to his conditioning being thrown off by the injury. His top secondary pitch is his changeup, a future plus pitch with good arm-side fade that took a large step forward late in the season. Howard's slider gives him a second plus pitch. It is a two-plane breaker, that can sometimes get a bit long and loopy. He still leans too much on his humpy curveball, which is at best an average pitch. It has been effective in the minors based on the velocity separation from the fastball, but advanced hitters will be able to read it out of his hand.

Howard repeats his delivery well, and has made big strides with consistency in pro ball. Like many young pitchers he is still working to fully make the move from control to command, but he has shown the ability to work his fastball up and his changeup to the outside of the zone.

The arm injury could have set back Howard's timetable for the majors, but the Phillies made sure he got plenty of innings in Double-A and the AFL to close the gap. He will compete for a spot out of the Phillies rotation to open the season, but the team has expressed a desire for him to get some work in with the major league ball in Triple-A before reaching the majors.

Variance: Medium. Howard has the stuff right now to step right into a major league rotation on Opening Day. The biggest knock against him is the lack of a sustained track record, and it is likely that early in the 2020 season the Phillies decide the stuff is too good to wait on the track record to develop.

Ben Carsley's Fantasy Take: Howard is exactly the type of fantasy pitching prospect you should be willing to get aggressive on. He's got legitimate SP3 upside, he figures to make an impact within the next season, and the scouting reports and numbers match up. Howard's arm injury and relatively limited track record of projecting as a dominant pitcher keep him out of the upper echelon of minor league fantasy arms, but he's firmly entrenched in the next group.

──────── ★ ★ ★ *2020 Top 101 Prospect* **#40** ★ ★ ★ ────────

2
Alec Bohm   3B   OFP: 60   ETA: 2020
Born: 08/03/96   Age: 23   Bats: R   Throws: R   Height: 6'5"   Weight: 225
Origin: Round 1, 2018 Draft (#3 overall)

The Report: We have a tendency as evaluators to make connections between prospects in the form of comparisons or comps. Players tend to be comped to others who look or feel the same, often in ways that show subtle (or not so subtle) biases. I try to stay away from comps as much as possible, but sometimes you just make a connection in your head.

So, with that disclaimer, Alec Bohm reminds me a lot of Maikel Franco as a prospect. It's not a visual comp; Bohm is a tall white kid from the Great Plains and Franco is a stout Dominican. It is a skill set comp in that they are both right-handed third basemen with limited range. Bohm's calling card is raw power that he hasn't quite translated into game power yet, and a potential plus hit tool that is far from locked in as plus. That looks a lot like Franco at the same stage. And, of course, Bohm is also seeking to replace the released Franco as the third baseman of the Philadelphia Phillies.

Franco has had enough of a major-league career that it's a bit much to call him a total bust, but he certainly never turned into the first-division regular that the Phillies hoped for. The similarities end at a certain point. Bohm already has a better plate approach than Franco ever developed, and Bohm's bat path is conducive to the adjustments that Franco never made. But Franco was once just about as touted a prospect as Bohm is now in a broadly similar form, and if nothing else it shows that there's some risk to the profile.

Variance: Medium. We believe in him as a major league regular, but there's a fair bit of variability in exactly how much power he hits for. He's also at some long-term risk of sliding off of third base to first or an outfield corner.

Ben Carsley's Fantasy Take: It would appear as though I'm more bullish on Bohm than my colleagues who know a lot more about him than I do. A normal human might take that as a sign he should recalibrate, but this is 2019, friends, and there's no time like the present to double down. Bohm is easily the best dynasty prospect in this org for my money, and while there's some risk attached to his profile in terms of future positional eligibility, I firmly believe he'll hit. We might not get truly star-level production out of Bohm, but I think he can get to .270 with 30-plus bombs and 3B eligibility at least into his late 20s. That'd make him a top-15 third baseman a la the 2019 iteration of Josh Donaldson.

3 Francisco Morales   RHP   OFP: 60   ETA: Late 2021
Born: 10/27/99   Age: 20   Bats: R   Throws: R   Height: 6'4"   Weight: 185
Origin: International Free Agent, 2016

The Report: The Phillies have done very well with five- and six-figure international free agent arms over the past decade. Morales is on the high side of that bonus range, but he's developing all the same. The projectability we've noted over the past few years finally manifested, as he was slinging it at 94-96 and bumping a tick or two higher in looks throughout the season. There might be a little projectability there left as a starter, and I'd expect the fastball to end up consistently in the high 90s if he moved to short relief. The slider is a plus pitch bordering on plus-plus, a true slider and a true out pitch. Those two weapons alone are enough to throw him into the 60 OFP conversation.

The usual concerns for the high-variance 60 OFP A-ball power pitcher profile are here too, of course. The changeup has developed faster than we thought it would a year or two ago, but that only gets it from fringy to fringe-average. Fringe-average is right on the border of being enough to give him a viable third pitch for a rotation, and a half-grade either way could make or break that. His delivery gives him some deception but also lends to repeatability problems. Because the Phillies employed a tandem system at Lakewood this year he never turned over the heart of the lineup a third time.

We could see the Phillies moving Morales to the bullpen as a fastball/slider guy, and we expect that he would be a quick mover with dominant late-game potential if they do. But the upside in the rotation might be too tantalizing…for the time being.

Variance: High, albeit typical. Adonis Medina had this sort of profile a few years ago and has stagnated a touch as he's moved up the chain. The changeup or command might never quite get all the way there. He just turned 20 and has yet to crack a hundred innings in a season.

Ben Carsley's Fantasy Take: For as special as Morales' arm can appear if you catch him on the right night, this is actually a fairly common dynasty prospect profile: Great Stuff (TM), but with substantial reliever risk and a so-so ETA. If you decide Morales is your dude among the glut of pitchers with similar profiles, that's totally reasonable. It's also reasonable to view him as a fringe-101 guy, as players with Morales' skill set bust in fantasy more often than they click.

4

Bryson Stott   SS   OFP: 55   ETA: Late 2021
Born: 10/06/97   Age: 22   Bats: L   Throws: R   Height: 6'3"   Weight: 200
Origin: Round 1, 2019 Draft (#14 overall)

The Report: The Phillies have taken a college hitter in the first round of the last three drafts, opting for safety over upside. In many ways Stott is similar to the first player of that group, Adam Haseley. Stott put up very good numbers in college, showing power, contact, and approach. The collection of tools are not overwhelming. His swing can get a bit long, and his bat speed is just average, leading to some questions about his long term ability to make contact at a high level. He has average power, mostly to his pull side. He may fill out and grow into more strength, but it is unlikely he will ever be much more than a 20-home-run-a-year hitter.

Stott's abilities in the field are similar to his abilities at the plate, more a collection of solid tools than anything stand out. He has enough range to stick at shortstop, and his hands are perfectly fine there. He has a bit of an awkward throwing motion that makes everything look not quite right, and his arm strength is slightly questionable, but still playable for the position. If he can't play shortstop full time, he could easily slide to second or third base and be a good defender at either.

The Phillies have been decently aggressive with their college players recently, and given Stott's polish he should start the year for High-A Clearwater, and should end the year in Double-A. His lack of upside means that he is probably that infielder that will move to a team's position of need than having a spot opened up for him.

Variance: Medium. Stott's collection of tools gives him a lot of safety, even if the tools don't all play to their ceiling. He does lose some value and ceiling if he has to move off of shortstop, but he should have plenty of glove, and just enough bat for second or third base.

Ben Carsley's Fantasy Take: First of all, this is a terrible name. Second of all, this is a weird-ass fantasy profile. I'm getting a hint of Jed Lowrie with…I think there are some notes of Paul DeJong? Then again, there's something about the aftertaste that denotes trace amounts of Joe Panik. Basically, Stott's value will hinge entirely on whether he can force his way into enough playing time to serve as an accumulator. That makes him an awfully tough dude to value from a dynasty standpoint, but tells you that you can stay away from popping Stott particularly early in your supplemental drafts.

5

Adonis Medina   RHP   OFP: 55   ETA: 2021
Born: 12/18/96   Age: 23   Bats: R   Throws: R   Height: 6'1"   Weight: 185
Origin: International Free Agent, 2014

The Report: With the Phillies shipping off Sixto Sanchez and Franklyn Kilomé, 2019 was supposed to be Adonis Medina's year to ascend to the top of the Phillies' pitching rankings. While the jump to Double-A is hard for most, it was particularly difficult for Medina. He regressed across the board, and his small frame seemingly struggled under the demands of a full-season workload.

If you gather the best of every Medina start, you can see the pitcher we projected him to be last year. However, he is now sitting in the lower end of his 91-96 fastball range, though he still shows the mid 90s. His changeup was trending towards plus, but it lacked sharpness and command. Starting in 2017, Medina had been phasing out a loopy curveball, for a sharp, hard slider, but it seems the two have mixed again into a loopy slider lacking bite. In addition to each individual pitch regressing, Medina's command has not improved, causing him to leave a lot of hittable pitches in the strike zone.

Medina still has mid-rotation upside if the Phillies can get him back to his pre-2019 path, and because of that they will likely return him to the Reading rotation to open the 2020 season. If the Medina's frame cannot hold up to the rigors of starting and maintain plus stuff, the Phillies may explore moving him to the bullpen where he may profile as a late-inning reliever.

Variance: High. The Adonis Medina that was on the mound for much of the 2019 season showed very ordinary stuff. If he cannot recapture his former stuff, he is just an ordinary reliever. However, Medina just finished his age-22 season and has some time still recapture his former prospect pedigree.

Ben Carsley's Fantasy Take: I'm too scared, basically. I wouldn't mind so much if Medina were just short, or just had some reliever risk, or was just coming off a down year. But combine all three and I think we've reached the point where Medina has more name value than actual value in dynasty formats right now. That's not to suggest you should sell low, but I wouldn't be diving into Medina stocks right now either.

Luis Garcia SS OFP: 55 ETA: 2023-24
Born: 10/01/00 Age: 19 Bats: B Throws: R Height: 5'11" Weight: 170
Origin: International Free Agent, 2017

The Report: We're not going to sugarcoat this: it was a rough season for Garcia. Playing the entire season at age-18, he jumped from complex ball all the way to full-season and he struggled badly. The switch-hitter was nearly pitcher-level useless from the left side, and only barely passable from the right side. He was overmatched, physically and developmentally. He'd probably have been better served spending the rainy months in Florida before heading to the Appy League, if only the Phillies *had* an Appy League affiliate.

Yet it wasn't a total loss. Surviving as an 18-year-old in full-season ball is, itself, an accomplishment. Garcia showed plus barrel control and a general feel for hitting even while not actually hitting much. There was a touch of bat speed on both sides, enough to project out that he's probably not going to be overmatched forever. He has keen defensive instincts and actions at the six spot and is likely to stay there or excel somewhere else on the dirt. It'll take some time, but there are still the makings of a regular shortstop here despite the ugly topline.

Variance: Very high. We don't know if he can hit yet. It's likely to be a few years before we know. He's very, very far away. Yet even if it takes a half-decade to sort everything out, he'll only be 23 during the 2024 season.

Ben Carsley's Fantasy Take: My issue is less with Garcia's full-season performance than it is that he was always a better real life prospect than a dynasty one. But between the long lead time, modest fantasy upside and recent track record, it's hard to make a case for Garcia as anything more than a prospect who'd rank in the 250-ish range at present. The Nationals' one is better.

7 **Mickey Moniak   OF**   OFP: 55   ETA: Late 2020
Born: 05/13/98   Age: 22   Bats: L   Throws: R   Height: 6'2"   Weight: 185
Origin: Round 1, 2016 Draft (#1 overall)

The Report: Prospect lists are an exercise in many things. One of those is expectations. When you draft a prep bat first overall amidst whispers of a plus or plus-plus hit tool, and he shows up and puts up a string of below-average offensive performances with muted scouting reports, it's a disappointment.

Moniak is not on track to develop an above-average hit tool, let alone a plus-plus one. He has subpar pitch recognition and ends up taking far too many off-balance hacks at spin that he can't hit. The plus barrel control that once spawned the lofty hit tool projections has let him survive through all of this, but it's hard to project major development there now. It's a long swing, and he hasn't shown many markers for future high averages since entering pro ball. What was once projected as his greatest strength is now a major weakness.

However, Moniak is still a solid prospect if you ignore his draft position and accept what he is now. He's grown into some thump, and we expect him to grow into at least average game power. He's a good athlete that runs well and can handle center. There's a very plausible outcome—indeed, it is the one we are giving him as his OFP—where he lands with a bunch of tools starting with the number 5 and ends up being a regular starting major league outfielder. It's not exactly what you want out of a 1-1, but it's not *bad*.

Variance: Medium. Moniak has a broad base of secondary skills that make him a likely reserve outfielder even if he misses a reasonable upside projection. It's been long enough that we're not assigning his former draft status much weight at all for potential positive variance, but your mileage may vary.

Ben Carsley's Fantasy Take: Few prospects in recent memory have had such wild fluctuations in dynasty value as Moniak. First, he was a top-50 dude based on his hit tool and draft position. Not too long after, every scouting report indicated you should drop him. And now, well, I wouldn't exactly call him a "buy low" candidate, but I think he has more value than you'd assume given the perception that he's a total bust. In fact, I'd argue that Moniak is probably a top-150 dynasty prospect; he's just got a very different profile than the one we hoped he'd have post-draft.

8 Johan Rojas OF
OFP: 55   ETA: 2023
Born: 08/14/00   Age: 19   Bats: R   Throws: R   Height: 6'1"   Weight: 165
Origin: International Free Agent, 2018

The Report: At some point I really want to write 3,000 words or so on MLB's plan for the minors. Unfortunately, I am in the midst of shepherding 30 team prospect lists, et. al., so it's going to be a while. And my thoughts on the plan are far more wide-reaching than "there'd have been no room for Johan Rojas under it," but I guess this will be my first salvo. Are the Phillies really making room for a diminutive, 17-year-old Johan Rojas as one of their 125 or 150 allowed contracted players? Are they dumping a 23-year-old, role 3 Double-A outfielder, one with enough speed-and-glove to have some up-and-down utility for a project like Rojas? Maybe, maybe not. They didn't have to make that calculation or one like it, and have developed a very nice outfield prospect as a result.

Rojas is a pure joy in center, a plus-plus runner who goes and gets it. He plays the outfield like a marauding strong safety, and he's built like one too, although in miniature. That frame will add good weight and he's already flashing plus raw in batting practice. The hit tool is raw, but he more than held his own as an 18-year-old in the Penn League, and was capable of the occasionally spectacular at the plate too. He's aggressive and the swing can get noisy generally or choppy against offspeed stuff, so the hit tool will take some time to develop. Fortunately, he has plenty of it, and the Phillies system is the better for it.

Variance: Extreme. There's hit tool questions here and he hasn't even reached full-season ball yet. As polished as the speed/glove part of the profile is at present, he may not end up with a true carrying tool.

Ben Carsley's Fantasy Take: Speed is relatively hard to come by in today's fantasy landscape, and that alone makes Rojas a decent add to your watch list. I'd be okay taking a flyer on him in leagues that roster 300-plus dudes, but anything shallower and you can probably wait and monitor for improvement. The hit tool risk and lead time are pretty big negatives for our purposes.

9 Damon Jones LHP
OFP: 55   ETA: 2020
Born: 09/30/94   Age: 25   Bats: L   Throws: L   Height: 6'5"   Weight: 225
Origin: Round 18, 2017 Draft (#533 overall)

The Report: We first flagged Jones as a sleeper very early in the 2018 season, when he was an interesting three-pitch pop-up lefty in Low-A. At the time, he was throwing 91-94 as a starter, although he'd thrown in the mid 90s previously in relief. In 2019, he was 93-96 in the rotation, which, along with a sharpening changeup and improved command, kicked him into a higher gear as a prospect. Jones dominated early on for High-A and blitzed through Double-A before running into the unfriendly Triple-A environment at the end of the season.

Jones is overaged for a 2017 college pick; he was drafted as a redshirt junior and turned 25 shortly after the 2019 season ended. We tend to care about age-relative-to-level less for talented arms than we do for bats, and his quick progress this past season certainly helps. But we do have to temper expectations some given that he's on the old side, and he's still a bit on the wild side, too.

Variance: Medium. There's a bit of risk in role, and there's a bit of further late development upside potential.

Ben Carsley's Fantasy Take: Jones is *probably* just a reliever, but the eye-popping strikeout numbers above tell me there's no harm in at least putting Jones on your watch list on the off chance the Phillies deploy him as a starter. There's pretty much zero buzz on Jones in dynasty circles as far as I can tell right now, so you should be able to take a wait-and-see approach without losing much sleep.

10 Rafael Marchan   C   OFP: 55   ETA: 2023-24
Born: 02/25/99   Age: 21   Bats: B   Throws: R   Height: 5'9"   Weight: 170
Origin: International Free Agent, 2015

The Report: Yes, the Phillies declined to protect Marchan from the Rule 5 Draft. No, that doesn't mean we're going to drop him out of our top ten prospects.

We repeatedly say that the primary basis of our prospect coverage is our live looks. We do actually mean that. We have many, many live looks at Marchan. I live close enough to Lakewood that I go to a couple dozen games a year there, and we had multiple full looks from other team members. All of our live looks on him were positive, and we got positive industry feedback on him too. He showed natural feel for hitting from both sides of the plate with potential for gap power. We like his defensive tools, although he's still inexperienced at the position and will need a good deal of work and time to develop.

The totality of that information would probably warrant a ranking a spot or two higher on this list. We aren't completely oblivious to the Rule 5 part of this, and this section of the list was tight enough that the protection information shaded Marchan down a spot or two. We also recognize that he's unprotected because he's a raw catcher with less than 100 games of full-season ball, and that is very tough to carry on an MLB roster unless you're egregiously tanking. (It wouldn't shock us at all to see one of those tanking teams take Marchan, actually.) We certainly think he's a better prospect than, say, Mauricio Llovera, but it's much easier to stick Llovera in an MLB bullpen right now than it is to carry Marchan as a reserve catcher. It's also much less of a big deal for the Phillies to start Llovera's option clock than Marchan's.

Variance: Extreme. He's an A-ball catcher and he's raw even by those standards.

Ben Carsley's Fantasy Take: You know how I feel about catching prospects by now, so you can probably guess how I feel about those described as "raw even by those standards." A hard pass for me.

The Next Ten

11 Simon Muzziotti   OF
Born: 12/27/98   Age: 21   Bats: L   Throws: L   Height: 6'1"   Weight: 175
Origin: International Free Agent, 2015

Muzziotti is one of the group of players signed by the Red Sox but then made free agents by MLB as a penalty for the Red Sox bundling of players to circumvent their bonus limit in 2016. Signed by the Phillies, he's made consistent progress as he has moved through the system.

At High-A Clearwater in 2019, the 20-year-old Muzziotti showed a quick and quiet swing and above-average plate discipline. He recognizes pitches well and uses the whole field. While his raw power is just average, Muzziotti finds gaps often enough to keep pitchers honest.

Muzziotti seems to understand the type of player he has to be in order to have success. He has an extreme ground ball approach, trying to take advantage of his plus speed. He is learning how to put that speed to use once he gets on base as well, improving his reads and jumps on the bases and creating enough distraction that pitchers have to be aware of him. He is becoming more comfortable stealing bases, though he still needs to improve his success rate.

Muzziotti uses his speed to his advantage in the field as well. He covers ground efficiently in center field and takes good routes to balls. His arm is strong and accurate enough to easily handle the position. Muzziotti is on a path—assuming continued improvement—to be a regular in center field.

12 Enyel De Los Santos   RHP
Born: 12/25/95   Age: 24   Bats: R   Throws: R   Height: 6'3"   Weight: 170
Origin: International Free Agent, 2014

The scouting report on Enyel De Los Santos has been pretty consistent for a few years now. At his best he will throw a fastball that spans the 90s, reaching up to 98, and back it up with an above-average to plus changeup and a collection of mediocre breaking balls. That seemed to be the report for most of the 2019 season, as De Los Santos continued to struggle to find a good breaking ball to step forward as a usable third pitch. His fastball command wavered, and at times his velocity fell more into the lower 90s. His struggles in Triple-A ultimately meant the Phillies didn't call him up as part of their September roster.

There is still a path forward where De Los Santos finds a slider or curveball that allows him to be a back end starting pitcher, but he has stagnated on the doorstep of that upside. At some point early in the 2020 season the Phillies are going to need to decide if they just want to move him to the bullpen and have him focus on being a fastball/changeup reliever.

13 Kendall Simmons   2B
Born: 04/11/00   Age: 20   Bats: R   Throws: R   Height: 6'2"   Weight: 180
Origin: Round 6, 2018 Draft (#167 overall)

Kendall (who went by Logan before changing it during the season) Simmons has a lot of positive traits going for him. The body is exactly what you like to see from a young high school draftee, lean with present muscle mass, but one you can still dream on adding more without losing his twitchiness. Present raw pop from above-average bat speed that can drive baseballs all over the field. The feel to hit is eh, the approach is very aggressive and can be exposed against arms with better sequencing. Defensively you don't really want him on the left side of the diamond given his lack of arm strength and first step quickness. He should be fine at second base, especially with all this shifting and such. This is kind of a boom or bust profile, one that might not work and get horribly exposed in full-season ball.

14 Cristopher Sanchez   LHP
Born: 12/12/96   Age: 23   Bats: L   Throws: L   Height: 6'5"   Weight: 165
Origin: International Free Agent, 2013

Back in early May, Sanchez was an intriguing arm in Extended Spring Training for the Rays, albeit as a 22-year-old who had spent three years in the DSL and was yet to crack full-season ball. Fast forward three months and Sanchez torched both A-ball levels and even earned a cameo appearance in Triple-A. So what happened? For one, the Rays have been notoriously aggressive in pushing guys if they believe they will hold their own and learn. Second, some guys just take longer to develop, especially taller kids. The fastball is plus at 92-94, the slider is firm with tilt, and the change has a chance to be plus with quality separation from his heater and big sink. Tampa Bay had too many quality prospects to protect everyone in December's Rule 5 draft, so they dealt Sanchez to the Phillies who had the 40-man space to protect this intriguing arm.

15 Victor Santos   RHP
Born: 07/12/00   Age: 19   Bats: R   Throws: R   Height: 6'1"   Weight: 191
Origin: International Free Agent, 2016

I like Santos more than this ranking. Despite not turning 19 until July, he was one of the best A-ball pitchers I saw in 2019, an advanced arm with pitchability who hardly ever walked anyone. He throws a split-change that is already above-average and should end up at plus. He mixes in a usable slider. The fastball comes in with strong run. The hitters usually tell you how effective a pitcher currently is, and Santos was consistently hard to square up in the Sally. Most of the individual pieces for future rotation success are already present.

The fastball velocity is missing, however. He sits around 90 and he was most often in the 88-91 band for me in Lakewood this year. That's teetering on the edge of not having enough velocity to be a serious prospect as a righty, and Santos looks close to maxed out. If he had a swing-and-miss breaking ball, I could probably justify blowing him up anyway, but he doesn't. I just don't know how many bats he's going to miss at higher levels. As precocious as he is, unless there's another trick up his sleeve he looks headed for fourth or fifth starter type of future.

16 JoJo Romero   LHP
Born: 09/09/96   Age: 23   Bats: L   Throws: L   Height: 5'11"   Weight: 190
Origin: Round 4, 2016 Draft (#107 overall)

Romero entered 2019 on the verge of majors, but his season got off to trouble from the start. His velocity was down in Spring Training, pitching more in the 89-91 range, and not his typical 93-94 when he was at his best in 2018. The Phillies still aggressively pushed him to Triple-A where he struggled mightily. He was eventually demoted to Double-A where he struggled less, and saw his command return some. At his diminished velocity and control, Romero projected more as an up-and-down starter than the low-end No. 3 starter upside he flashed at times.

The Phillies moved Romero to the bullpen for the Arizona Fall League, and while his strikeouts weren't up, he was dominant and his velocity was back near his peak, leading to the Phillies protecting him on the 40-man roster. At his best, Romero has an above-average fastball, a plus changeup, and two average breaking balls. None of that projects to be a dominant reliever, but he should be able to handle a multi-inning role and provide a similar impact as Ranger Suarez did in 2019. If he manages to get most of his stuff back together, he could still be a back end starting pitcher.

17 Connor Seabold   RHP
Born: 01/24/96   Age: 24   Bats: R   Throws: R   Height: 6'2"   Weight: 190
Origin: Round 3, 2017 Draft (#83 overall)

The Phillies have turned to the Cal State Fullerton well many times in the draft or trades during recent years. Seabold has more stuff than most of his college rotation mates, but he is not going to blow hitters away either. The Phillies smoothed over his delivery in late 2018, ditching a Bronson Arroyo-esque leg kick for a more repeatable and consistent motion. An oblique injury delayed the beginning of Seabold's season until June 25, and it was August before he was throwing full starts, causing the Phillies to send him to the Arizona Fall League to get him to 73 1/3 innings.

Seabold's fastball sits in the low 90s, and can get it up to 94-95. He backs it up with a solid curveball and an average changeup. He has above-average control and solid command, allowing his full arsenal to play up. His ceiling is still fairly modest, as he projects more as a solid No. 4 starter, but he should open the year in Triple-A and could see the major leagues before the end of the 2020 season.

18 Nick Maton   SS
Born: 02/18/97   Age: 23   Bats: L   Throws: R   Height: 6'1"   Weight: 165
Origin: Round 7, 2017 Draft (#203 overall)

Maton is likely not a future all-star, but he is becoming an interesting player. He has soft hands, good range, and good footwork. His arm would play anywhere in the infield. While he looks to be able to handle a regular gig at shortstop, his future is more likely that of an up-the-middle utility guy with solid defense and good on-base skills.

Offensively, Maton is patient and disciplined with a short swing that is quick to the ball and allows for a lot of contact. He starts from an open stance and uses a toe tap to get his timing and squares himself up and he reacts well to offspeed pitches. He doesn't project for a lot of power and he hits a lot of balls on the ground to make use of his speed, but he would help himself if he looked to use more of the field as he currently hits too many balls to the pull side.

Maton has better than average speed and can steal a base. While he does seem like a utility player long-term, whether that is an old school utility guy or more of a modern, everyday utility guy will likely depend on how much he can wring out of that hit tool.

19 Kyle Glogoski   RHP
Born: 01/06/99   Age: 21   Bats: R   Throws: R   Height: 6'2"   Weight: 183
Origin: International Free Agent, 2018

Going into 2019, the only reason you might've come across Glogoski would be that he is from New Zealand, one of the Phillies' diverse international signees (this includes players from Russia, Taiwan, China, France and Saudi Arabia). He was fine in my 2018 looks. He commanded a fastball, big loopy curveball and a changeup that was his most effective swing-and-miss pitch. In 2019, he started in Extended Spring Training but then finished making 11 starts in High-A Clearwater. As part of the Phillies carousel of piggybacked arms in Lakewood, Glogoski was called up and proceeded to dominate the level, forcing a move to face stiffer competition. The fastball doesn't light up the gun, settling in at average, but he knows where to put it, consistently going inside and getting awkward swings. The curveball is still not especially sharp, but he can mix it in as a change of pace offering. The changeup jumped over the last year and is now his best offspeed pitch. It mirrors his fastball and has late dive, almost like a split, and he uses it to both sides of the plate. Without a swing-and-miss breaker at present, Glogoski can be vulnerable against better hitters as he climbs, but for now, as the ambassador for New Zealand baseball, he is fun.

20 **Erik Miller LHP**
Born: 02/13/98   Age: 22   Bats: L   Throws: L   Height: 6'5"   Weight: 240
Origin: Round 4, 2019 Draft (#120 overall)

Miller was the Phillies fourth-round pick in the 2019 draft, and it is easy to see why some viewed him as a steal. In college, Miller was up to 97 with a plus slider from the left side, but it is also easy to see why he fell to where he did. His velocity was often inconsistent, and his command was poor. In professional ball, the Phillies have worked on cleaning up his delivery to improve his control. The result has been that Miller has been working more comfortably in the 90-94 range, but with a much higher strike rate. He backs the fastball up with a slider that, when consistent, is a plus pitch. His changeup has also shown as an above-average pitch in the past.

The Phillies have had luck building big pitchers with arm strength back up in the past, and Miller could experience a jump like Damon Jones did this year, at which point his ceiling is mid-rotation starting pitcher. If the control issues come back, the Phillies may be forced to move Miller to the bullpen and hope the velocity comes back and he can work as a two-pitch reliever.

Personal Cheeseball

Deivy Grullon C
Born: 02/17/96   Age: 24   Bats: R   Throws: R   Height: 6'1"   Weight: 180
Origin: International Free Agent, 2013

We flagged Grullon as a potential Rule 5 pick last year as a major-league-ready catcher with a simple swing and surprising pop. He didn't get popped then, but he did get added to the Philadelphia 40-man as a September call-up off a strong Triple-A campaign. He's hit 21 homers in each of the last two seasons, though the 2019 homer output was just as assisted by the juiced Triple-A ball as the 2018 output was by Reading's generous confines. Grullon brings along a strong defensive reputation fueled by a rocket throwing arm, but he hasn't graded out well by our upper-minors framing metrics. He profiles as a fun backup catcher with power upside, and could take over that role for the Phillies in 2020.

Low Minors Sleeper

Starlyn Castillo RHP
Born: 02/24/02   Age: 18   Bats: R   Throws: R   Height: 6'0"   Weight: 210
Origin: International Free Agent, 2018

Signed for a $1.6M bonus in the '18 signing period, Castillo's stateside debut was unspectacular and marred by false starts. He didn't pitch much during Extended Spring Training or in the GCL due to a myriad of ailments and injuries. When he did pitch, the results weren't great, but that can likely be chalked up to rust and inconsistency. You can see why he got so much money, with clean arm action, arm speed, a big heater, and swing-and-miss breaker. There are present signs of concern, given that the body has already softened up, he wasn't that "projectable" to begin with, he missed time in his first pro year, and he lacks feel for the strike zone. But, this is a 17-year-old kid with stuff that gets your attention and who still has a long developmental path in front of him.

Top Talents 25 and Under (as of 4/1/2020)

1. Scott Kingery
2. Spencer Howard
3. Alec Bohm
4. Adam Haseley
5. Zach Eflin
6. Francisco Morales
7. Bryson Stott
8. Seranthony Dominguez
9. Adonis Medina
10. Luis Garcia

The Phillies are a win-now team, with most of their core either in their traditional prime years, or 30ish free agent signings. Scott Kingery is eligible by a month, and followed up a disastrous rookie campaign with a solid sophomore bounceback. He's traded off some hit for power, but the pop plays—baseball contingent I suppose—and he's a quality defender at several spots, and passable at several more. He may only settle in as a solid-average regular, but that kind of production with that much defensive flexibility is a valuable piece in 2020 baseball.

As a prospect, Adam Haseley never really popped as much as you'd want an eighth-overall pick to. There's strong tweenerish markers in the profile, but he's useful at three outfield spots—although how useful depends a lot on your defensive metric of choice—and there's average hit/power projection in the bat. There's strong fourth outfielder/Role 45 vibes so far, but he's MLB-ready with upside past that, which is something the prospect names behind him can't really say.

Zach Eflin is the pitcher version of that profile and slots in right behind Haseley. He's league averageish the past two seasons, although DRA likes him less than RA or FIP metrics, and he's not quite durable/efficient enough or quite good enough to pencil him into your Opening Day rotation. There's a good chance he ends up there anyway though.

Seranthony Dominguez would be ahead of Haseley and Eflin if he weren't dealing with a small UCL tear. He's a potential dominant late inning reliever if healthy. His offseason should be normal, but elbow injuries are…well, not what you want.

Part 3: Featured Articles

The Baseball Is Juiced (Again)

Robert Arthur

This article originally appeared at Baseball Prospectus on April 5, 2019.

It started when the normally reliable Chris Sale got lit up for three homers by the Mariners in the Red Sox's season opener. It was part of a record number of taters that flew on Opening Day, as starters from Sale to Zack Greinke were taken deep by the handful. Then Christian Yelich hit a home run in each of his first four games, tying yet another MLB record, this one for consecutive games with a dinger to start a season.

It didn't take long for fans and players to begin whispering and tweeting about the baseballs being juiced again. It's early yet for us to come to any definitive conclusion about the 2019 season, but preliminary data shows that the baseball has returned to its aerodynamic peak. Whether that means this season will smash home run records like 2017 did remains to be seen.

Before home run explosion over the last few years, no one worried too much about the baseball's air resistance. While MLB and Rawlings (the company that manufactures the official baseballs) kept track of dozens of metrics to make sure that the ball was consistent from month to month, they didn't measure drag.

But drag is incredibly important in determining how likely a hitter is to knock one out of the park. As baseballs become more aerodynamic, they travel further given a certain initial velocity. A deep fly ball that might have been caught at the warning track can instead go into the first row of the stands. A three percent change in drag coefficient can work to add about five feet to a well-hit fly ball, which can in turn increase home runs league wide by an astounding 10-15 percent.

It's possible to measure the aerodynamics of the baseball using the pitch-tracking radars currently in place in each MLB ballpark. By calculating the loss of speed from when the pitch is released to when it crosses the plate, you can directly measure the drag coefficient on the baseball. I first wrote about the role of decreasing drag in boosting home runs in 2017, and MLB's commission of scientists and statisticians later confirmed that the more aerodynamic baseballs in use that year were largely to blame for the spike in home runs. The same commission rejected some alternate hypotheses, like rising temperatures and a league-wide boost in launch angle pushing more balls over the fence.

The current era has featured some large fluctuations in drag coefficient, leading to first an explosion in 2016 and 2017, and then a dialing back of homers last year. Curious about the record-breaking home run tallies in the last few days, I used the same methodology to measure the aerodynamics of the baseballs so far in 2019.

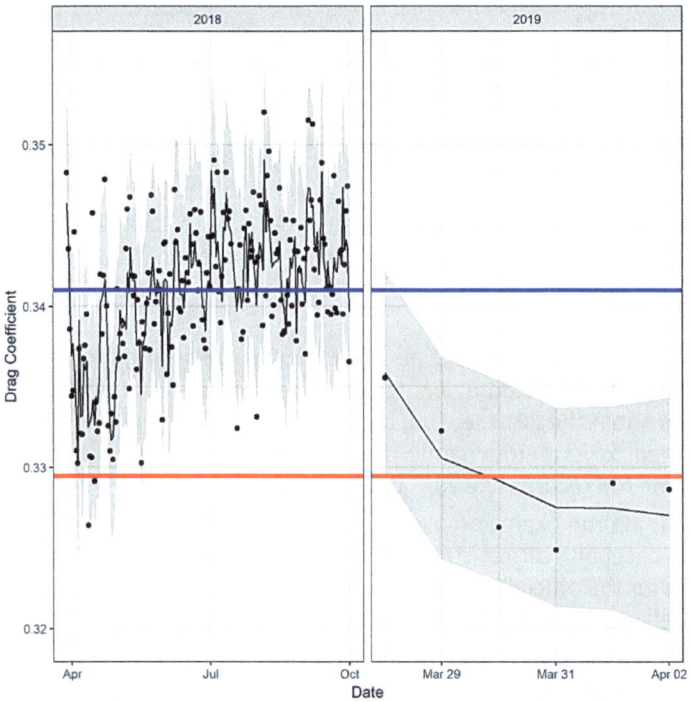

We're only a week into the 2019 season, but the drag numbers so far are among the lowest recorded in the last calendar year. With apologies for gory math, the current 2019 season average drag coefficient (the red line) would be below the 95 percent credible interval (the shaded area) for about nine-tenths of the 2018 season. (I used a Bayesian Random Walk model implemented in INLA to calculate these credible intervals, averaging the drag numbers in each game and adjusting for park.)

There were only a handful of six-day stretches in 2018 that had drag numbers below what we're seeing now, and most were in late June and early July. All of this means that 2019's data so far is quite a bit different than what we saw through most of last year.

These drag coefficients factor out the effects of temperature and air density, so they aren't a product of April cold. However, the numbers could be deceptive if the radars used to track pitches have changed from year to year. I consulted with some experts within baseball who were not aware of any specific modifications to the radar this year that could produce this pattern, but it's an important caveat of which to be aware.

On the one hand, it's only been six days, and we don't quite have the statistical basis to say that these drag coefficients are unprecedented compared to 2018. On the other hand, we've witnessed about 5,000 fastballs so far this season, so it's not as if our sample size is small. At least so far, the baseball has played like it's much more aerodynamic than it was last year. In fact, the current drag coefficient is really only comparable to 2017, when the baseballs were more aerodynamic than they had been in at least a decade.

It's not just fancy radar tracking indicating that the baseball is flying through the air more easily. The current number of home runs per game (as of this writing) is the highest it's been since the heady days of 2017, the year that teams and players broke dinger-related records everywhere you looked. That's especially remarkable considering that we're in what is typically the coldest part of the regular season, when lower temperatures and higher winds tend to suppress offense and keep balls in the air within the park. Comparing only from April to April, this year's rate of home runs per fly ball is even a little bit higher than it was in 2017.

With that said, the current measurements are no guarantee that 2019 will be another year of record-shattering homer hitting. The trouble with the drag measurements is that they are not consistent from June to August, from week to week, or even sometimes from day to day. Whether because of natural manufacturing variation or differences in the underlying supplies of cowhide and thread that go into the baseballs, drag has a tendency to fluctuate up and down over the course of a year. So the homers that fly in the first week of April wouldn't necessarily clear the fence a week later.

It's possible that this one-week drop in drag coefficient subsides and the baseball returns to its 2018 levels. On the other hand, it's almost equally probable that the ball becomes even more slippery and flies ever farther. Either way, it's clear that the baseball's air resistance is something to keep an eye on for the remainder of the 2019 season.

—*Robert Arthur is an author of Baseball Prospectus.*

The Moral Hazard of Playing It Safe

Craig Goldstein

This article originally appeared at Baseball Prospectus on August 6, 2019.

A couple days prior to the trade deadline, amidst a sea of tranquility posing as the lead up to the trade deadline, Bob Nightengale took to Twitter. Nightengale, who was probably wearing his pants backwards at the time, tweeted that MLB GMs were coming around on the idea that the unified trade deadline should be moved back from July 31 to August 15, so they could better assess their positions in the standings and whether they should buy or sell. To which I said:

This might strike some as reductive and churlish. And it might be that, but it isn't really wrong, either. Jeff Quinton wrote a great piece discussing the environmental factors that enable front offices to avoid risk without upsetting the apple cart within their own fanbases. I don't believe that it goes far enough, however. His article gives us the proper framework through which to understand why these behaviors have been allowed to seep into front offices throughout the league. Understanding the reasons behind these actions are different from excusing them, though, and GMs should not be let off the hook for their non-competitive approach to the trade deadline (much less the offseason).

⚾ ⚾ ⚾

It's fair to say that fans as a group have rarely, if ever, been pro-player. It is also fair to say that in the time during and following the Moneyball revolution, the pendulum swung from fans who cared intensely about winning in the moment (and thus might be intolerant of a rebuilding approach) to fans who supported building a team that could compete throughout multiple seasons, viewing the playoffs as a crapshoot, with the thought that getting multiple bites at the apple was a better approach than taking a bigger bite in any one season.

There's nothing wrong with that approach, and I still find merit in that argument. However, it seems that the pendulum has swung too far in that direction. Teams are overvaluing some of the individual factors that make themselves long-term contenders rather than attempting to seize a championship when given the opportunity. It's a difficult needle to thread.

And surely, they (and those in similar positions) would have liked another two weeks to clarify where they stand so as to better marshal their resources. We've all asked for a few more minutes when staring at a menu. But all of these GMs and front office personnel are where they are to make difficult decisions. They have proprietary data and internal analysts dedicated to understanding their position relative to the rest of the league, and how any move in the here and now impacts their long-term vision. To complain (if that report is accurate) that over half the season is not enough to properly assess their season is bullshit of the highest order. Move the deadline, and you'd simply have increasingly discounted trade offers because teams would be acquiring even less control of anyone they're acquiring, rental or not.

Major league front offices are behaving like the managers they lampooned two decades ago. They're effectively sacrificing a runner to second in the ninth inning—not because it's the correct move, but rather because it is safe. It used to be that the phrase "moral hazard" was used to describe general managers who made ill-fated, short-sighted decisions aimed at locking in wins and securing their jobs at the expense of their team's future. Now, general managers are guilty of committing moral hazards in the opposite direction, playing it utterly safe and terrified of becoming scapegoats.

In lieu of bold action, they opt to pussyfoot around a current window of contention, choosing instead to play the long game and stack up years of control like they're blocks in a game of Jenga. GMs pass on signing quality players in free agency because the back-end of the deal might look bad, and because they might be able to squeeze out 70 percent of the production from a player who costs a tenth as much. That's a safer investment, too, because it's also hard to prove a negative—it's impossible to prove that Manny Machado would make the Mets a playoff team in 2019-2020, but it's easy to say that the back half of Robinson Cano's contract sucks. Owners, who rule over GM's jobs, are also humans with human brain processes that will always make the so-called albatross contract uglier than the road not taken.

These days, GMs are remembered for the bad deals they make and the surplus value they generate, not the acquisition of expensive, necessary talents that meet their market worth (or fall slightly short while still providing significant on-field value). And front offices know that one or two expensive misfires can cost them their jobs, no matter how many good deals they make.

No front office exemplifies this ethos more than the Toronto Blue Jays. General Manager Ross Atkins had this to say following the Blue Jays underwhelming trade deadline:

This is by no means the first time that an executive will cite years of control to justify their actions, which is often just another way of saying "don't look at what we got, look at how much we got of it." Atkins touts quantity to elide the discussion of quality—either, that of the players acquired, or those given up. Remember: the other teams presumably value years of control, too.

Atkins also had some thoughts to offer regarding free agents back in early 2018:

This ignores, of course, whether the player can create enough value in the front end of a contract to justify the longer term of a deal, and the decline that often occurs in the back end. It also ignores whether the player can fill a need the team requires and put them in a position to compete for and win a championship. But as teams seemingly avoid contention at all, where they might end up having to consider and later justify some of these tough decisions, we still see risk-averse approaches.

Anthony Fenech's article on two trades that recently extended GM Al Avila didn't make got at this issue rather well:

> Passing on those deals was defensible: Both players had yet to break out and trading [Michael] Fulmer—a pitcher who appeared to be a future ace, no matter his injury concerns—would have taken serious gumption, opening Avila up to strong criticism.

Avoiding strong criticism is something each of us can understand as a motivation, but the avoidance of criticism only matters if that criticism is valid. In Fulmer's case, shoving his injury concerns aside affects not only the years that the team controls him (he is currently missing a full season due to Tommy John surgery) but also the quality of those seasons, as his knee and elbow injuries combined to dampen his effectiveness even when healthy enough to pitch. But it was easy to present the then-current image of Fulmer as a top of the rotation pitcher who the team had under its domain for the next five seasons as something to build around. The status quo isn't nearly as often second-guessed as a decision that disrupts it.

⚾   ⚾   ⚾

MLB GMs are risk-averse to a fault. They are ivy-educated and consulting firm-approved, and yet they can't seem to avoid leaving wins on the table in their all-consuming lust for a non-existent $/WAR championship. They are supposed to zig when everyone else zags, and not merely pay lip service to the idea of zigging through a calculated PR plan built on convincing the fan base their approach is novel when it actually apes most of their competitors. Instead they've become far more concerned with making safe, accepted-by-the-new-common-wisdom decisions, such that our prior understanding of what a moral hazard is has become inverted.

I can't blame them entirely, and not only because of the reasons that Quinton illuminated in his article, but also because of the damage wrought by the introduction of the second wild card (WC2) spot. MLB's desire to have more teams in playoff contention has sparked anti-competitive behavior. Teams know now that they do not need to swing big as they assemble their roster because there is a good chance that a mediocre team can either catch fire and capture a division, or muddle along until they back into the WC2.

Simultaneously, the one-game playoff has neutered the WC1, putting an entire season on the flip of a coin like some sort of baseball-obsessed Anton Chigurh. While the one-game playoff makes sense as a way to increase the value of winning a division, it also means that if a front office doesn't like its chances of overcoming a behemoth like the Dodgers or Astros in the offseason, they have few incentives to chase glory. Similarly, the relative inaction in the NL Central at the trade deadline—despite a wide open division—can be explained by the idea that any high-variance investment could still result in only a wild card (or worse) result, given the mere two months left in the season to make an impact.

⚾   ⚾   ⚾

As stated at the top, we should not confuse reasons for excuses. The implementation of the second wild card is just one of many environmental factors that influence how each front office operates. I am convinced that it is one of the larger factors, but I am also convinced that organizations need to shed the yoke of "efficiency at all costs" so that they can instead pursue competition, as the spirit of the game intends. Until they do, we're all deadline losers.

—*Craig Goldstein is an author of Baseball Prospectus.*

Index of Names

Álvarez, José 89
Anderson, Drew 103
Arano, Victor 103
Arrieta, Jake 57
Bohm, Alec 91, 106
Brito, Daniel 101
Bruce, Jay 24
Castillo, Starlyn 117
Cleavinger, Garrett 103
Davis, Austin 103
De Los Santos, Enyel 95, 113
Domínguez, Seranthony 59
Eflin, Zach 61
Gamboa, Arquimedes 101
Garcia, Edgar 103
Garcia, Luis 92, 109
Garlick, Kyle 26
Glogoski, Kyle 116
Gosselin, Phil 101
Gregorius, Didi 28
Grullon, Deivy 101, 117
Hammer, J.D. 103
Harper, Bryce 30
Harrison, Josh 33
Haseley, Adam 35
Herrera, Odúbel 37
Hoskins, Rhys 39
Howard, Spencer 96, 105
Hundley, Nick 101
Hunter, Tommy 103
Irvin, Cole 103

Jones, Damon 97, 111
Kelley, Trevor 103
Kingery, Scott 41
Knapp, Andrew 101
Liriano, Francisco 63
Llovera, Mauricio 103
Mahtook, Mikie 101
Marchan, Rafael 101, 112
Martini, Nick 43
Maton, Nick 101, 116
McClain, Reggie 65
McCutchen, Andrew 45
Medina, Adonis 98, 108
Miller, Erik 103, 117
Moniak, Mickey 93, 110
Morales, Francisco 99, 107
Morgan, Adam 67
Morrison, Logan 101
Muzziotti, Simon 101, 113
Neris, Héctor 69
Neshek, Pat 103
Nola, Aaron 71
Ortiz, Jhailyn 101
Parker, Blake 73
Pirela, Jose 101
Pivetta, Nick 75
Quinn, Roman 47
Realmuto, J.T. 49
Rivera, T.J. 101
Robertson, David 77
Rodriguez, Sean 101

Philadelphia Phillies 2020

Rojas, Johan	....	101, 111	Straily, Dan	 103
Romero, JoJo	....	100, 115	Suárez, Ranger	 79
Sanchez, Cristopher	....	103, 114	Swarzak, Anthony	 81
Santos, Victor	....	114	Torreyes, Ronald	 101
Seabold, Connor	....	115	Vargas, Jason	 83
Segura, Jean	....	51	Velasquez, Vince	 85
Simmons, Kendall	....	114	Walker, Neil	 53
Stock, Robert	....	103	Wheeler, Zack	 87
Stott, Bryson	....	94, 108	Williams, Nick	 55